best ever

vegetarian

This is a Parragon Publishing Book
This edition published in 2004

Parragon Publishing
Queen Street House
4 Queen Street
Bath BA1 1HE
United Kingdom

Created and produced by
The Bridgewater Book Company Ltd,
Lewes, East Sussex

Photographer Ian Parsons
Home economists Sara Hesketh & Richard Green

ISBN: 1-40541-690-4

Printed in China

NOTE

This book uses imperial and metric measurements. Follow the same units
of measurement throughout; do not mix imperial and metric. All spoon
measurements are level: teaspoons are assumed to be 5 ml and tablespoons are
assumed to be 15 ml. Unless otherwise stated, milk is assumed to be whole milk,
eggs and individual vegetables such as potatoes are medium, and pepper is freshly
ground black pepper.

The times given for each recipe are an approximate guide only because
the preparation times may differ according to the techniques used by
different people and the cooking times may vary as a result of the type of oven
used. Ovens should be preheated to the specified temperature. If using a fan-
assisted oven, check the manufacturer's instructions for adjusting the time and
temperature. The preparation times include chilling and marinating times,
where appropriate.

The nutritional information provided for each recipe is per serving or per portion.
Optional ingredients, variations or serving suggestions have not been included
in the calculations.

Recipes using raw or very lightly cooked eggs should be avoided
by infants, the elderly, pregnant women, convalescents, and anyone
suffering from an illness.

contents

introduction

Essential to good health, vegetables are abundantly available and delicious. Nowadays, there is a huge variety of vegetables on sale in local food stores and street markets and everybody is sure to find some that suit their palate. They are full of vitamins and minerals—they can contribute up to half of the recommended daily intake of vitamin C and a quarter of the recommended intake of vitamin A, as well as folic acid and vital substances such as calcium.

Vegetables are good for everyone. The nutrients they contain boost the immune system and improve our general health. Studies have suggested that the dietary fiber they provide may help to reduce the risk of cancer, especially in the digestive system. Improved digestive health shows on the outside, leading to thicker, shinier hair, clearer skin, and loss of excess weight.

Vegetables contain a high proportion of water and very few calories—it's the additional butter and creamy sauces that make them fattening. Most contain almost no fat or oil and are ideal for those trying to lose weight. For people on a low-salt diet, vegetables can be a blessing, as they are usually very low in sodium. Most vegetables are also low in dietary cholesterol, and the fiber they contain may help to lower blood cholesterol levels.

magical medley

A huge range of fresh vegetables are available all year round. They can be included in every meal—even breakfast. You can experiment with hundreds of different types of vegetables and with different methods of cooking. If you are lucky enough to have a Caribbean or Chinese market near you, talk to the stallholder, who will usually gladly share information on how to prepare and cook unfamiliar vegetables. If you do not like a vegetable cooked one way, try preparing it differently—roast carrots instead of boiling them, eat cabbage raw in coleslaw instead of boiling it, stir-fry cauliflower instead of baking it with a sauce. For breakfast, try broiled mushrooms, broiled tomatoes, or Bubble & Squeak (see page 64).

Whatever your tastes and preferences, the dishes featured in the following pages will whet your appetite. There are dishes to suit every occasion—some low fat and others more indulgent. For a picnic, try Mushroom & Onion Quiche (see page 78); for a hearty breakfast, create a Spanish Omelet (see page 93). Phyllo Pockets (see page 127) and Dauphinois Potatoes (see page 158) will be a hit at a dinner party, and Vegetarian Lasagna (see page 120) makes a delicious family supper.

children, vegans, and meat-eaters

If you are cooking for children, try Minestrone (see page 23) or Sesame Stir-Fry (see page 189) if you are short of time, or Cauliflower Cheese Surprise (see page 72) if the pantry is looking bare—a favorite with kids.

All of the recipes contained in this book are ideal for vegetarians, and many can be adapted to use your favorite vegetables, but if you are a meat-eater, you can add a little meat or fish to many of the dishes. Vegetables will go well with anything, including cheese, eggs, pasta, grains, and meat or fish. You can add flavor and color with sauces and dressings.

Many of the recipes are suitable for vegans—this is indicated in the recipe introduction. These dishes contain no animal products whatsoever, and they can be eaten on their own or as an accompaniment to another dish for meat-eating families.

types of vegetable

There are many different types of vegetable. For ease of reference, the various vegetables featured in this section are split into groups.

brassicas: This group of vegetables provides an excellent source of vitamin C. Broccoli works well combined with other vegetables and with cream or cheese sauces. When buying broccoli, look for dark green or purple flowers with no yellowing. Choose firm stems, store in the refrigerator and use within two days. Trim off small florets, leaving a little stem if you like. Discard the main stem and any leaves. Cut the florets into even-size pieces to cook. Broccoli is best steamed or stir-fried to preserve its stores of folic acid, vitamin A, and potassium.

Brussels sprouts are rather like baby cabbages. Store in the refrigerator, loosely wrapped, for a few days. They are too strongly flavored to be eaten raw and are best lightly steamed, sautéed, stir-fried, or boiled and tossed in butter. Cut a cross in the stem before cooking.

Cabbage and kale are also brassicas. Their outer leaves may be a little damaged, but check the inner leaves—these should not be bruised or yellowed. Cabbage should feel heavy and firm. Store in the refrigerator, loosely wrapped, for only a few days. Cabbages deteriorate once cut, and lose their firm texture and nutrients. To prepare, discard any damaged outer leaves and cut out the core (cabbage) or any tough ribs (kale). Slice into thin strips to steam or into thicker pieces to boil. Cook until the color brightens but the vegetable is still firm to the bite. Whole white cabbage leaves are great stuffed and baked, or washed and shredded for coleslaw. To preserve the color of red cabbage, add a little vinegar to the cooking water. Braise slowly in as little water as possible.

Chinese cabbage has a more delicate flavor. Look for pale, crisp leaves when buying. Store in the refrigerator, loosely wrapped, for a few days. Discard the outer leaves before cooking. Stir-fry, sauté, or use raw in salads.

Cauliflower comes in many varieties, ranging from white to pale green and purple. Choose cauliflowers with outer leaves, as these protect the more delicate flowers. The flowers should have no brown spots and should be tight, not opened-out, which is a sign that the vegetable is past its best. Store in the refrigerator for a few days. Prepare like broccoli, cutting into small florets. Steam, sauté, boil, or stir-fry for a short time—if overcooked, it becomes soggy and smells unpleasant. Cauliflower is traditionally served with dairy products, such as cheese sauce, but can also be served raw in bite-size pieces with hummus. Hummus with Crudités (see page 41) makes an excellent appetizer.

Kohlrabi tastes like a cross between turnip and cabbage and is slightly peppery. Choose kohlrabi with smooth skin and store in the salad drawer of the refrigerator for up to two weeks. Remove any protruding stems before cooking. Peel with a small, sharp knife, as the skin is too tough for a vegetable peeler. Place the cut pieces in a bowl of water acidulated with lemon juice. To cook, steam, microwave, or boil.

leafy greens: Vegetables in this group may be red or purple rather than green. Most of them are strongly flavored and very versatile.

Chinese greens are related to brassicas. Some of the best known are bok choy, mustard greens, and Napa cabbage. Look for colorful leaves with no signs of wilting. Store in the refrigerator and use within two days. Chop or slice small leaves; if you are using larger leaves, chop the leaf and rib separately. To cook, stir-fry, steam, or sauté.

Spinach and Swiss chard go particularly well with dairy products and are also good in Asian dishes, as they pair happily with chile, ginger, and other Asian flavors. When buying spinach, look for dark leaves with lots of color and without yellowing or bruising. Swiss chard should also have dark leaves and white or red stems—it is like spinach, but has a milder flavor and thicker stems. Store in the refrigerator for no more than two days. Rinse spinach and Swiss chard in several changes of water and pat dry. Both contain large amounts of water—cook about twice as much of the raw vegetable as you actually want to eat, as the volume will reduce dramatically. Slice Swiss chard stems crosswise and cook separately. Both vegetables are tastiest steamed or stir-fried.

stalks and buds: This group includes artichokes, asparagus, celery, Belgian endive, and fennel. These vegetables vary in flavor, texture, and cooking methods.

The globe artichoke, a member of the thistle family, is ideal for people who don't mind a little mess. Try cooking them and using just the hearts or use canned artichoke hearts. Roasted artichokes preserved in oil are also available. When buying fresh, look for bright color and firm, tightly packed heads. Brown spots at the bottom of the head indicate that an artichoke is past its best. Eat as soon after purchase as possible, or store in the refrigerator overnight, wrapped in damp paper.

When preparing artichokes, have a bowl of water acidulated with lemon juice ready to place the cut pieces in, as they yellow quickly. To cook whole, break off the stem and trim the bottom flat. Trim the spines, cut off the top, then boil in water with salt and lemon juice for 35 minutes. It is ready when the leaves come away easily when gently pulled. Drain upside down. Eat one leaf at a time, dipping the fleshy part in vinaigrette or melted butter and discarding the remainder. When the fleshy leaves have been pulled off, remove the pale leaves and scrape away the choke (the thick white fibers) with a knife—the heart which remains can be eaten.

To prepare an artichoke for stuffing, remove the stem and some of the outer leaves. Trim and cut across the top, about a third of the way down. Boil as above, then remove the internal leaves and scrape away the choke with a spoon, leaving a hollow cup to stuff.

Baby artichokes are also available. These can be eaten whole. Cook for about 12 minutes. Young, fresh baby artichokes can be eaten raw.

Asparagus is delicious and features in many dishes, from risotto to stir-fries. Choose firm spears with tightly closed tips—they may be white or green—and eat within a day of purchase. To prepare asparagus, trim off any woody ends and cut into bite-size pieces, or leave whole. Steam, boil, broil, roast, or stir-fry and serve with melted butter or to complement another dish.

Celery adds texture to salads and stir-fries and makes a good crudité. It will keep for about a week in the refrigerator. To prepare, separate the stalks and rinse under cold running water. Remove and discard the leaves, unless using as a garnish, and pull away any strings. Slice thinly for stir-fries, or leave whole to serve with hummus.

Belgian endive goes well with butter and cheese, as it has a bitter taste and crunchy texture. It can be flavored with herbs and lemon juice and goes well with walnuts. Select crisp heads with pale leaves that are yellow at the top. Before cooking, remove any damaged outer leaves. To eat raw in salads, slice the vegetable or separate the whole leaves. To cook, blanch the whole vegetable to reduce the bitterness, chop it, then broil, stir-fry, or sauté.

Fennel has a distinctive aniseed taste. It goes well with Mediterranean flavors such as tomatoes and basil, but will also complement fruit, onions, or spinach. Choose firm, evenly colored bulbs with bright green fronds. Store in the refrigerator for up to a week. To cook, trim the bottom and cut off woody stems. Slice thinly to add to soups or casseroles or eat raw in salads. Fennel is also delicious broiled, steamed, or roasted.

salad greens: Many different vegetables fall into this category, from lettuce, cress, mizuna, and arugula to more exotic ingredients such as escarole and radicchio.

Butterhead lettuce is a round lettuce with soft leaves and a delicate flavor. Iceberg and romaine have little flavor, but with their crisp texture they keep for a relatively long time in the refrigerator. Boston lettuce is smaller and sweeter than romaine. The purple Lollo Rosso and green Lollo Biondo taste slightly bitter, but look attractive. Oak leaf lettuce, a loose-leaf variety, also looks attractive, with purple edges and darker coloring inside.

Cress has a hot flavor, and can be added to soups and casseroles as a garnish or flavoring. Mizuna has a spicy taste and dark green feathery leaves. Arugula has a peppery flavor and slender, bright green leaves.

Escarole, frisée, and radicchio provide a range of tastes, from tangy to quite bitter. They are best used sparingly, mixed with other greens. The deep red color and white ribs of radicchio make it especially attractive.

Choose fresh greens with no bruising or wilting. Remove plastic packaging as soon as you get home and store in the refrigerator. Some mixed salad greens are packaged in plastic bags for freshness and should be left as they are. Once you have opened the bag or cut the vegetable, use the greens as quickly as possible.

To prepare salad greens, gently wash in cold water and pat dry without breaking or bruising them. Tear the greens instead of chopping them—this prevents bleeding of the juices and preserves more of the vegetable's nutrients. Some varieties, such as romaine lettuce, are coarser and do need to be chopped or shredded. If you are adding a salad dressing, do so just before serving, because pouring dressing over the salad too early may cause it to go soggy. Leafy salads are best lightly drizzled with plain olive oil or a light vinaigrette. Try adding other ingredients, such as cheese, croutons, toasted nuts, or pitted olives. Alternatively, try creating traditional dishes such as Caesar Salad (see page 210).

other salad vegetables: In summer, salad vegetables are plentiful and inexpensive. The following examples combine well with a variety of salad greens.

Avocados are actually classed as fruit rather than vegetables, but are used in savory dishes. They have a high fat content. Ripe avocados will feel soft when gently pressed. Most stores sell avocados that will take two or three days to ripen, and these will feel hard. Do not use an unripe avocado and do not store in the refrigerator. To speed up ripening, store in a paper bag at room temperature for a day. To prepare, cut lengthwise around the stone. Ease the halves apart and remove the stone. Brush lemon juice on the flesh to prevent discoloration. Eat with mayonnaise or vinaigrette, or remove the flesh and mash to make guacamole. To add to salads, peel off the skin and slice the flesh.

Cucumber has a very high water content and mixes well with strongly flavored ingredients to give a cooling effect. Look for firm cucumbers with no soggy patches. Store in the refrigerator and cut as you need it, discarding the first dried-out slice. For a quick and easy dip, cut cucumber into small cubes and mix with plain yogurt, garlic, chopped fresh mint, and a little snipped fresh dill. When used in recipes like this, it is best salted first to draw out excess moisture. Sprinkle the chopped cucumber with salt and let stand in a colander for one hour before patting off the salt with paper towels.

The peppery flavor and crunchy texture of bite-size red or white radishes make them ideal for salads. They can be eaten whole or thinly sliced. They can also be cut decoratively and used as an attractive garnish. Store in the refrigerator for up to one week.

mushrooms: A huge variety of mushrooms are available today, both fresh and dried. Some exotic varieties have become so popular that they are now being cultivated. You may be lucky enough to live somewhere where they grow wild—but if you pick exotic mushrooms, make sure that you can identify edible varieties accurately. Cultivated white mushrooms are the most widely available. They have a neat appearance and work well used whole.

They will hold their shape if sliced and added to casseroles or stir-fries and can be used to make soups, although you may favor more strongly flavored mushrooms for this purpose.

Ceps, also known as porcini, are available fresh and dried and have a fine flavor. The dried varieties are best when a strong flavor is required in soups or stocks. Chanterelles have a delicate flavor and golden appearance. Brush off dirt rather than washing them, as they are very porous.

Paris and cremini mushrooms are very similar and have firm textures and strong flavors. They are ideal for adding flavor to stuffings, pie fillings, or sauces. Portobello mushrooms are large and tasty and are best served plain. Roast, stuff, and bake, or wrap in foil and grill.

Morel mushrooms are becoming increasingly popular. Although most fresh mushrooms should only be wiped with damp paper towels, these are the exception, as their texture traps dirt. Soak morels in salted water for a couple of minutes to remove any insects, then rinse under cold running water and pat dry. Use whole or sliced.

Oyster mushrooms are sold fresh and have an attractive fluted shape. Usually grey, there are also pale pink or yellow varieties. Oyster mushrooms can be used in most dishes, but release a lot of moisture during cooking.

Shiitake mushrooms, originally native to Japan, are now grown in many other countries. They have a chewy texture and robust flavor. Slice thinly for stir-fries and sauces and cut into chunks for casseroles. If using dried shiitake mushrooms, reconstitute in boiling water and reserve the water for stock. Straw mushrooms, native to China, are cultivated on straw. They are small and similar to white mushrooms, and are usually available in cans.

When buying fresh mushrooms, make sure they are firm with no bruising or brown patches or any signs of moisture. Exotic mushrooms will deteriorate faster than cultivated varieties, so use them quickly. Dried exotic mushrooms can be expensive, but you need only very small quantities as they have a strong flavor and will swell to about four times their original weight. It is worth buying dried mushrooms for sauces or soups unless you have access to fresh, strongly flavored exotic mushrooms. Store in a cool, dry place, away from delicately flavored foods that may absorb their strong aroma.

To prepare fresh mushrooms, wipe cultivated varieties and gently brush the dirt from exotic mushrooms. Trim away any woody stems. Soak dried mushrooms in wine, stock, or water before use. This helps to remove trapped dirt. If you use hot liquid, soak for about 20 minutes, but extend the time if you use cold liquid. Remove the mushrooms, then strain the liquid and use it for stock.

peas and beans: These vegetables add a splash of color to casseroles and salads, and they freeze well, making them quick and easy to prepare. Peas are available frozen and fresh, although the fresh season is short. They are tasty in curries and creamy pasta dishes. Buy fresh pea pods that are full, plump, and a bright color. Store in the refrigerator for up to three days. Press the bottom of each pod to open it and push the peas out using your thumb. Fresh peas have the best texture if they are lightly steamed, boiled, microwaved, or added to stir-fries.

Snow peas and sugar snap peas are very similar to one another, although the latter are plumper. The pods are eaten whole, and have a crunchy texture. Look for firm, crisp pods with bright coloring. Store in the refrigerator for three or four days. To cook, break off the stems and peel the strings from the sides. Cut diagonally into bite-size pieces and stir-fry or steam.

When buying fresh beans, look for good color. Long beans such as green beans should snap in half if they are fresh, unless they are young or small varieties. Asian yard-long beans may have patches on them; these will disappear when they are cooked. Store in the refrigerator for four or five days. Fava bean pods may look leathery, but the beans inside will be fine. Choose medium-size pods with a good color. Store in the refrigerator for three or four days. To prepare, remove the beans from the pods and cook in boiling water for about 5 minutes for young, small beans, and about 15 minutes for older, larger ones.

corn: Corn can be eaten on the cob or as kernels. Choose cobs completely enclosed in green husks, with plump kernels. Eat as soon as possible after purchase as the corn will lose its sweetness. Store in a plastic bag in the refrigerator for up to two days. To prepare, remove the outer leaves and the silks, then boil in water, or steam, for 10 minutes. The kernels should feel tender when pierced. To strip the cob, hold it at an angle and scrape off the kernels with a sharp knife, working down and away from yourself. One cob provides about 4 oz/ 115 g of kernels. Baby cobs are ideal for casseroles, stir-fries and stews. They can also be steamed or sautéed.

the onion family: The vegetables of this family are essential for flavoring many dishes, and can also be cooked on their own. Standard brown onions are useful, all-purpose vegetables. The Spanish onion is a large, white-fleshed variety with a mild flavor. White onions have crisp flesh and are tasty raw or cooked. Red onions add color to dishes, and are good for broiling and roasting. Onions from warmer climates are usually sweeter than those from colder countries.

When buying onions, look for firm bulbs and evenly colored skin with no sprouting. Store in a cool, dry, dark place and they will last from a few weeks to a few months, depending on the variety—red and sweet onions do not keep as long as brown onions. Cut off the ends and peel off the skin before chopping and cooking.

Garlic is also part of the onion family. It is thought to have health benefits, helping to lower blood cholesterol levels and boosting the immune system. Choose firm bulbs with no cuts or slits. Stored in a cool and airy place away from moisture, garlic will keep for several weeks. To prepare, peel and chop it, then crush it with the blade of a knife, or use a garlic press. Avoid burning garlic when cooking, as it makes the dish bitter. Roasted garlic makes an attractive garnish and adds a subtle flavor to salad dressings and dips. Roast large, unpeeled cloves in a preheated oven, 400°F/200°C, for about 5 minutes. Cool before peeling.

Shallots are smaller than onions and have a milder, sweeter flavor. The flesh is sometimes pink. Look for firm bulbs when buying. Store for up to a month in a cool, dry place. Prepare and cook in the same way as onions.

Leeks have a milder flavor than onions. They go well with cheese sauces and potatoes. Choose small to medium leeks for the best texture and look for dark green, healthy leaves. Stored in the refrigerator, leeks will keep for up to a week. To prepare, remove the outer leaves, trim both ends and cut lengthwise along the green part, almost to the white part. Rinse well under cold running water, fanning out the leaves to remove any dirt trapped inside. Cut into slices or chunks and stir-fry, bake, broil, sauté, or roast.

Scallions are used most often in salads and stir-fries. The leaves should look bright and not wilted and should have no hint of yellowing. Store in the refrigerator for up to a week. Trim both ends and remove any damaged outer leaves. Chop, slice, or cut into lengths and stir-fry, or add raw to salads for texture and flavor.

roots and tubers: This group of vegetables should be peeled thinly, as much of their nutritional content is located just below the skin. They also begin to lose their vitamin C when stored longer than about a week. Avoid buying vegetables that are sprouting.

Beets taste sweet and go well with onion or citrus flavors, tangy cheeses, and mustard or horseradish. Buy firm, smooth bulbs, with leaves attached. Separate the leaves and store in the salad drawer in the refrigerator for up to a few weeks. To prepare, scrub the roots, then roast, bake, boil, or eat raw— grated or thinly sliced.

Carrots go with many different flavors, from spicy curry dishes to mild cheese sauces. They will keep for about a week in a cool and airy place. Peel thinly unless they are organically grown. Trim both ends and slice or dice, then boil, steam, microwave, stir-fry, or roast.

Celery root tastes like celery. It goes well with cheese, butter, or cream cheese and is tasty raw in salads. Buy medium-size vegetables—larger ones tend to be woody or hollow. Peel off the skin and place cut pieces in water acidulated with lemon juice. To cook, boil or sauté.

Jerusalem artichokes have a sweet flavor and crisp flesh. Use in soups and stews, or serve with sour cream. Buy firm tubers without blemishes. Store in the salad drawer in the refrigerator for up to two weeks. Use immediately if they begin to sprout. To prepare, scrub and peel. To avoid discoloration after peeling, place them in a bowl of water acidulated with lemon juice (do not let them stand for too long before cooking). To cook, bake, roast, boil, steam, or sauté.

Parsnips have a strong, sweet flavor, but cannot be eaten raw. Choose small, firm parsnips and store in a cool, dry place for up to a week. To prepare, scrub, peel, trim, and slice or chop, then boil, steam, sauté, or roast.

Potatoes are one of the most widely grown vegetables in the world. Use waxy varieties for boiling, sautéeing, and salads, and floury varieties (which have a higher starch content) for baking and mashing. Do not use green potatoes, as they contain toxins caused by exposure to light, although small green patches can be cut out. Stored in a dark, dry, well-ventilated place, potatoes will keep for about two weeks. To prepare, scrub or peel thinly to remove pesticides, then boil, roast, or bake.

Sweet potatoes have dark orange or pink flesh (these are known as yams) or white flesh. Their sweet flavor makes them ideal for casseroles or purées. Store in a cool, dry place for up to a week. To cook, scrub and bake, or peel thinly, chop, boil, and mash.

Turnips have greenish-white or purple skin and a peppery flavor. Choose small, smooth-skinned turnips and avoid any with shrivelled roots. Store in a cool place for up to two weeks. Scrub young turnips under cold running water; older turnips need peeling. Add to casseroles or steam, sauté, or mash.

Caribbean yams are similar to the sweet potato, although more starchy. Check for rotten patches when buying and store in a cool, dry, dark place for up to a week. Scrub, rub with oil, and bake whole.

fruit vegetables: The nutritious vegetables in this group add color to a range of dishes. Eggplants are very versatile. They should look smooth and glossy. Store in a cool, dry place. To prepare, wipe, trim the top, and slice or dice. Roast, or add to dishes such as moussaka.

Chiles vary in heat from mild to extremely hot. Generally, the more innocent-looking the chile, the hotter it is: small, dark chiles are usually the hottest. Habanero is one of the hottest and Anaheim one of the mildest. Red chiles are usually sweeter than green varieties. Store for up to three weeks in the refrigerator. They keep well in a jar of oil. Wear gloves when handling chiles, as the oils permeate the skin. Always wash your hands well after handling them and before touching your eyes or mouth. The membrane and flesh around the seeds are the hottest parts of a chile, and can be removed before cooking.

Sweet bell peppers commonly come in green, red, yellow, and orange varieties and are related to chiles, although they are not spicy. White and purple varieties are available. The warmer the color, the sweeter the bell pepper. Red and yellow bell peppers are good sources of vitamin C. When buying bell peppers, look for firm, smooth skins and bright colors. A mix of colors on one bell pepper is perfectly acceptable. Store in the salad drawer in the refrigerator for up to a week. To prepare, slice off the top and bottom of the bell pepper, cut the remainder in half, then remove the seeds and membrane. Slice into strips or chop. If you are planning to stuff the bell pepper, slice off the top and pull out the core, shake out any remaining seeds, and cut out the membrane. Add to casseroles or stir-fries, broil or roast, bake whole, or eat raw in salads.

Summer squashes include zucchini, and patty pan and yellow crookneck squash. Buy medium-size, firm, glossy vegetables, with no wrinkled or brown patches. Store in the refrigerator, loosely covered, for three or four days. Summer squashes should not be peeled, as they lose their flavor and become soggy. Wipe or rinse, and trim the ends. Chop large vegetables and stuff, steam, or add to casseroles. Summer squashes are delicious roasted.

Winter squashes and pumpkin are great for soups and casseroles and keep for months in a cool, dry, well-ventilated place. They go well with cheese, hot spices, and strong flavors, such as garlic. Once cut, wrap and store in the refrigerator and use quickly. To cook, peel varieties with thick skins, then boil or steam, or leave the skin on and roast or bake.

Tomatoes are the best known of the fruit vegetables. They should feel firm, but not rock hard. Red tomatoes are ripe; yellow ones need a few more days (unless they are a yellow variety). Cherry tomatoes are bite-size and have a sweet flavor. They are particularly attractive in salads. Store at room temperature: they will keep for a few days if ripe, a few more if unripe. Wipe before using, then chop or slice and broil, bake, or roast.

basic recipes

rich unsweetened pastry dough

makes: 1 x 9-inch/23-cm tart shell
preparation time: 10 minutes,
plus 30 minutes chilling

1¼ cups all-purpose flour
pinch of salt
⅓ cup butter, plus extra for greasing
1 egg yolk
3 tbsp iced water

1 Sift the flour and salt into a bowl. Add the butter, cut it into the flour, then rub in with your fingertips until the mixture resembles breadcrumbs.

2 Beat the egg yolk with the water in a small bowl. Sprinkle the liquid over the flour mixture and mix with a round-bladed knife or your fingertips.

3 Form the dough into a ball, cover, and chill for 30 minutes.

mayonnaise

makes: 1¼ cups
preparation time: 15 minutes

2 egg yolks
pinch of salt, plus extra for seasoning
⅔ cup sunflower oil
⅔ cup olive oil
1 tbsp white wine vinegar
2 tsp Dijon mustard
pepper

1 Beat the egg yolks with a pinch of salt. Mix the oils in a jug. Gradually add one-quarter of the oil mixture, a drop at a time, beating constantly with a whisk or electric mixer.

2 Beat in the vinegar, then continue adding the oils in a steady stream, beating constantly.

3 Stir in the mustard and season to taste with salt and pepper.

pizza doughs

makes: 2 x 10-inch/25-cm pizzas
preparation time: 20 minutes,
plus 1 hour rising

2½ cups strong white bread flour, plus extra for dusting
1 tsp salt
generous ¾ cup lukewarm water
2 tbsp olive oil, plus extra for greasing
1 tsp active dry yeast

1 Sift the flour and salt into a large, warmed bowl and make a well in the center. Add the water, oil, and yeast to the well. Using a wooden spoon or your hands, gradually mix to form a dough.

2 Turn out on to a lightly floured counter and knead for 5 minutes, or until smooth and elastic. Form the dough into a ball, place in a clean, lightly oiled bowl, and cover with oiled clingfilm. Let stand in a warm place to rise for 1 hour, or until doubled in bulk.

3 Turn the dough out on to a lightly floured counter and knock back. Knead the dough briefly before shaping into 2 x 10-inch/25-cm circles.

vegetable stock

makes: 8 cups
preparation time: 20 minutes
cooking time: 45 minutes

2 tbsp corn oil
4 oz/115 g onions, finely chopped
4 oz/115 g leeks, finely chopped
4 oz/115 g carrots, finely chopped
4 celery stalks, finely chopped
3 oz/85 g fennel, finely chopped
3 oz/85 g tomatoes, finely chopped
9¼ cups water
1 bouquet garni

1 Heat the oil in a large pan. Add the chopped onions and leeks and cook over low heat, stirring occasionally, for 5 minutes, until softened.

2 Add the remaining vegetables, cover, and cook over very low heat, stirring occasionally, for 10 minutes. Add the water and bouquet garni, bring to the boil, and simmer for 20 minutes.

3 Sieve, cool, and store in the refrigerator. Use immediately or freeze in portions for up to 3 months.

crêpe batter

makes: 12 crêpes
preparation time: 10 minutes,
plus 30–60 minutes resting (optional)

generous ¾ cup all-purpose flour
salt
1 egg, lightly beaten
1¼ cups milk
1 tsp corn oil

1 Sift the flour with a pinch of salt into a bowl. Using a wooden spoon, beat in the egg and half the milk. Continue beating until the mixture is smooth and lump free.

2 Stir in the remaining milk and the oil.

3 Pour the batter into a pitcher and, if you have time, let stand for 30–60 minutes. Stir the batter before cooking the crêpes.

soups & appetizers

Vegetable dishes are often the preferred choice for appetizers, even when the main course will be fish or meat, as they offer such variety and really do tempt the taste buds. Soups are wonderfully versatile, too, and many of the recipes here, such as Broccoli & Cheese Soup (see page 21) and Creamy Tomato & Basil Soup (see page 26), would make a tasty light lunch served with some fresh crusty bread, as well as a delicious first course. This chapter includes some familiar classics, such as Minestrone (see page 23), some more unusual recipes, such as Pear & Watercress Soup (see page 20), and a choice of chilled soups, such as Gazpacho (see page 32), for alfresco dining in the summer.

Recipes for vegetarian appetizers take their inspiration from cuisines across the world. Take a gastronomic tour from Italian Antipasti (see page 38), through Mexican Frijoles (see page 35), to Turkish Imam Bayildi (see page 49). Dishes range from hot and spicy to smooth and creamy. Some are simplicity itself, while others are elegant and sophisticated enough for a formal dinner party. Some do not involve any cooking at all, while others are served warm or piping hot.

Whether you are a committed vegetarian or vegan, or just looking for something a little different and interesting, you are sure to find exactly the right recipe to set your taste buds tingling.

french onion soup

⏱ **cook: 1 hr 30 mins**   ⏲ **prep: 30 mins**   **serves 6**

variation

If you like, you can stir 2 tablespoons of brandy into the soup just before ladling it into the bowls.

Simple, but perfect, this flavor-packed soup could be served as an appetizer or a light lunch. French onion soup is traditionally made with chicken or beef stock, but this version, suitable for vegetarians, is based on a rich, tasty vegetable stock made with onions, leeks, carrots, celery, fennel, and tomatoes.

INGREDIENTS

1 lb 8 oz/675 g onions

3 tbsp olive oil

4 garlic cloves, 3 chopped and

1 peeled but kept whole

1 tsp sugar

2 tsp chopped fresh thyme

2 tbsp all-purpose flour

½ cup dry white wine

8 cups Vegetable Stock

(see page 13)

6 slices French bread

3 cups grated Swiss cheese

fresh thyme sprigs, to garnish

cook's tip

Make sure that you allow yourself plenty of time to make the Vegetable Stock (see page 13) in advance of making the soup. If you let the stock stand, the flavors will have more time to develop.

1 Thinly slice the onions. Heat the olive oil in a large, heavy-bottomed pan, then add the onions and cook, stirring occasionally, for 10 minutes, until they are just beginning to brown. Stir in the chopped garlic, sugar, and thyme, then reduce the heat and cook, stirring occasionally, for 30 minutes, or until the onions are golden brown.

2 Sprinkle in the flour and cook, stirring, for 1–2 minutes. Stir in the wine. Gradually stir in the Stock and bring to a boil, skimming off any scum that rises to the surface, then reduce the heat and simmer for 45 minutes. Meanwhile, toast the bread on both sides under a preheated medium broiler. Rub the toast with the whole garlic clove.

3 Ladle the soup into 6 flameproof bowls set on a cookie sheet. Float a piece of toast in each bowl and divide the grated cheese between them. Place under a preheated medium–hot broiler for 2–3 minutes, or until the cheese has just melted. Garnish with thyme and serve.

spicy dhal & carrot soup

serves 6   **prep: 15 mins**   **cook: 45 mins**

This soup uses split red lentils and carrots as the two main ingredients and includes a selection of spices to give it a kick. It makes a nutritious meal in itself, combined with some crusty bread. The lentils are high in fiber and protein, and the carrots are a good source of vitamins C and E.

INGREDIENTS

⅔ cup red split lentils

5 cups Vegetable Stock (see page 13)

12 oz/350 g carrots, sliced

2 onions, chopped

8 oz/225 g canned chopped tomatoes

2 garlic cloves, chopped

2 tbsp ghee or vegetable oil

1 tsp ground cumin

1 tsp ground coriander

1 fresh green chile, seeded and chopped, or 1 tsp crushed chile

½ tsp ground turmeric

1 tbsp lemon juice

salt

1¼ cups milk

2 tbsp chopped fresh cilantro

plain yogurt, to serve

NUTRITIONAL INFORMATION	
Calories	173
Protein	9g
Carbohydrate	24g
Sugars	11g
Fat	5g
Saturates	1g

variation

Try using just ½ a teaspoon ground cumin and ½ a teaspoon ground coriander, and add 1 teaspoon curry powder, for a slightly different taste.

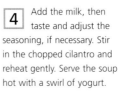

cook's tip

Simmer the lentil mixture on a fairly low heat to make sure that it doesn't stick to the bottom of the pan, otherwise it may start to burn.

1 Place the lentils in a strainer and rinse well under cold running water. Drain and place in a large, heavy-bottomed pan with 3½ cups of the Stock and the carrots, onions, tomatoes, and garlic. Bring to a boil, then reduce the heat, cover, and simmer for 30 minutes, or until the vegetables and lentils are tender.

2 Meanwhile, heat the ghee in a small skillet. Add the cumin, ground coriander, chile, and turmeric and cook over low heat for 1 minute. Remove from the heat and stir in the lemon juice. Season to taste with salt.

3 Process the soup in batches in a blender or food processor. Return the soup to the pan, add the spice mixture and the remaining Stock, and simmer over low heat for 10 minutes.

4 Add the milk, then taste and adjust the seasoning, if necessary. Stir in the chopped cilantro and reheat gently. Serve the soup hot with a swirl of yogurt.

pear & watercress soup

This is a creamy and sophisticated soup that may be served hot or chilled (see Cook's Tip). It is traditionally made with chicken stock, but this vegetarian version substitutes good-quality vegetable stock.

INGREDIENTS

4 pears

1 bunch of watercress
or 3½ oz/100 g arugula

scant 3½ cups Vegetable Stock
(see page 13)

juice of ½ lemon

salt and pepper

½ cup heavy cream

CROUTONS

2–3 slices of day-old white bread

2 tbsp olive oil

NUTRITIONAL INFORMATION	
Calories	136
Protein	.................1g
Carbohydrate	.........11g
Sugars	..............11g
Fat	.................10g
Saturates	.............6g

cook's tip

To serve chilled, let the soup cool before stirring in the cream in Step 4, then transfer the mixture into a bowl, cover with plastic wrap and chill in the refrigerator for 1–2 hours.

 Core and slice the pears. Reserve one-third of the watercress leaves. Place the remaining leaves and stems in a pan and add the pears and Vegetable Stock. Bring to a boil, then reduce the heat and simmer for 15 minutes.

 Meanwhile, make the croutons. Cut the crusts

 off the bread, then cut the bread into ¼-inch/5-mm squares. Heat the olive oil in a heavy-bottomed skillet and add the bread cubes. Cook, tossing and stirring constantly, until evenly colored. Drain on paper towels.

3 Remove the pear and watercress mixture from the heat, let cool slightly, then

 add the reserved watercress leaves. Pour into a blender or food processor and process until smooth. Push the mixture through a fine-mesh strainer into a bowl with the back of a wooden spoon. Stir in the lemon juice and season to taste with salt and pepper.

4 Stir in the cream and return the soup to the

clean pan. Heat gently until warmed through, then serve immediately, garnished with the croutons.

broccoli & cheese soup

cook: 20 mins　　　　**prep: 20 mins**　　　　serves 6

This richly flavored soup is popular with adults and children alike and, served with some crusty whole-wheat bread, is substantial enough to make a satisfying lunchtime snack.

NUTRITIONAL INFORMATION

Calories	249
Protein	. . . . .14g
Carbohydrate	. . . . .16g
Sugars	. . . . .4g
Fat	. . . . .15g
Saturates	. . . . .9g

INGREDIENTS

2 fresh tarragon sprigs

2 tbsp butter

1 onion, chopped

1 lb/450 g potatoes, peeled and grated

salt and pepper

7 cups Vegetable Stock

(see page 13)

1 lb 9 oz/700 g broccoli,

cut into small florets

6 oz/175 g Cheddar cheese

1 tbsp chopped fresh parsley, plus

extra to garnish

cook's tip

Do not overfill the blender or food processor. When you are making a large quantity of soup, you may need to process it in several smaller batches.

1 Chop enough tarragon to fill 2 teaspoons. Melt the butter in a large pan. Add the onion and cook, stirring occasionally, for 5 minutes, or until softened. Add the grated potatoes and tarragon, season to taste and mix. Pour in just enough of the stock to cover and bring to a boil. Reduce the heat, cover, and simmer for 10 minutes.

2 Meanwhile, bring the remaining stock to the boil in a separate pan. Add the broccoli and cook for 6–8 minutes, or until tender.

3 Remove both pans from the heat, let cool slightly, then ladle the contents of both pans into a blender or food processor. Process until smooth, then pour the mixture into a clean pan. Grate the cheese, stir it in with the parsley, and heat gently, but do not let it boil. Ladle into warmed soup bowls, garnish with extra chopped parsley, and serve immediately.

minestrone

cook: 2 hrs 15 mins　　**prep: 40–45 mins**　　**serves 6**

variation

To make Minestrone alla Genovese, substitute pesto for the grated Parmesan cheese in Step 3.

There are as many variations of this classic Italian soup as there are Italian cooks. You can use almost any vegetable in season to make minestrone, and if you are a meat-eater, you can add a little chopped pancetta or lean bacon to the mix.

INGREDIENTS

2 fresh basil sprigs	2 carrots, chopped
2 fresh marjoram sprigs	2 potatoes, chopped
2 fresh thyme sprigs	1 small turnip, chopped
2 tbsp olive oil	1 celery stalk, chopped
2 onions, chopped	¼ small cabbage, shredded
2 garlic cloves, chopped	2 oz/55 g dried stellette or other
4 tomatoes, peeled and chopped	soup pasta shapes
½ cup red wine	salt and pepper
7 cups Vegetable Stock	2 tbsp freshly grated Parmesan cheese,
(see page 13)	plus extra for serving
⅔ cup Great Northern beans, soaked	
overnight in cold water, then drained	

cook's tip

If you are a meat-eater you can add 2 slices of pancetta, or Italian bacon, rinded and chopped, to the soup in Step 1. It is available from Italian delicatessens and adds an extra depth of flavor to the soup.

1 Chop enough fresh basil, marjoram, and thyme to fill 2 tablespoons and reserve until required. Heat the olive oil in a heavy-bottomed pan. Add the onions and cook, stirring occasionally, for 5 minutes, or until softened. Stir in the garlic and cook for an additional 3 minutes, then stir in the chopped tomatoes and the reserved herbs.

2 Add the wine, simmer for 1–2 minutes, then add the Stock and drained beans. Bring to a boil, then reduce the heat, partially cover, and simmer for 1½ hours.

3 Add the carrots, potatoes, and turnip, then cover and simmer for 15 minutes. Add the celery, cabbage, and pasta, then cover and simmer for an additional 10 minutes. Season to taste with salt and pepper and stir in the Parmesan cheese. Ladle into warmed bowls and serve with extra Parmesan cheese.

stilton & walnut soup

serves 4　　　　　**prep: 10 mins** ⏱　　　　　**cook: 30 mins** 🍲

Full of flavor, this rich and creamy soup is very simple to make and utterly delicious to eat, making it a memorable dish, ideal for serving to adventurous guests. It is packed with protein, and if served with bread makes a very filling meal.

INGREDIENTS

4 tbsp butter	5½ oz/150 g blue Stilton cheese,
2 shallots, chopped	crumbled, plus extra to garnish
3 celery stalks, chopped	2 tbsp walnut halves,
1 garlic clove, crushed	coarsely chopped
2 tbsp all-purpose flour	⅔ cup plain yogurt
2½ cups Vegetable Stock	salt and pepper
(see page 13)	chopped celery leaves, to garnish
1¼ cups milk	

NUTRITIONAL INFORMATION

Calories 392

Protein 15g

Carbohydrate 15g

Sugars 8g

Fat 30g

Saturates 16g

---

variation

Substitute diced or grated apple for the celery leaves for an alternative garnish that will help to bring out the flavors of the cheese and walnuts.

  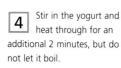

cook's tip

As well as adding protein, vitamins, and useful fats to the diet, nuts add important flavor and a crunchy texture to vegetarian meals.

---

1 Melt the butter in a large, heavy-bottomed pan. Add the shallots, celery, and garlic and sauté, stirring occasionally, for 2–3 minutes, or until softened.

2 Reduce the heat, add the flour, and cook, stirring, for 30 seconds, then gradually stir in the Stock and milk and bring to a boil.

3 Reduce the heat until the mixture is gently simmering, then add the crumbled blue Stilton cheese and walnut halves. Cover the pan and simmer for an additional 20 minutes.

4 Stir in the yogurt and heat through for an additional 2 minutes, but do not let it boil.

5 Season the soup to taste with salt and pepper, then transfer to a warmed soup tureen or individual serving bowls. Garnish with chopped celery leaves and extra crumbled blue Stilton cheese.

creamy tomato & basil soup

serves 6   **prep: 20 mins**   **cook: 30–35 mins**

Use plum tomatoes for this summery soup, if possible, as they are less watery and have a more intense flavor than standard ones. It will be even more delicious if they have ripened on the vine.

INGREDIENTS

2 tbsp butter

1 tbsp olive oil

1 onion, finely chopped

1 garlic clove, chopped

2 lb/900 g plum tomatoes, chopped

generous 2¾ cups Vegetable Stock (see page 13)

½ cup dry white wine

2 tbsp sun-dried tomato paste

salt and pepper

2 tbsp torn fresh basil leaves

⅔ cup heavy cream

fresh basil leaves, to garnish

NUTRITIONAL INFORMATION

Calories	.234
Protein	.2g
Carbohydrate	.8g
Sugars	.6g
Fat	.21g
Saturates	.11g

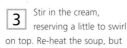

cook's tip

Double cream does not usually curdle, but may do when combined with acidic ingredients. This is why the soup should not be allowed to boil once the cream has been added.

1 Melt the butter with the oil in a large, heavy-bottomed pan. Add the onion and cook, stirring occasionally, for 5 minutes, or until softened. Add the garlic, tomatoes, Stock, wine, and tomato paste, stir well, and season to taste. Partially cover the pan and simmer, stirring occasionally, for 20–25 minutes, or until the mixture is soft and pulpy.

2 Remove the pan from the heat, leave to cool slightly, then pour into a blender or food processor. Add the torn basil and process. Push the mixture through a strainer into a clean pan with a wooden spoon.

3 Stir in the cream, reserving a little to swirl on top. Re-heat the soup, but do not let it boil. Ladle the soup into warmed bowls, add a swirl of the reserved cream to each, garnish with the basil leaves, and serve immediately.

crécy soup

cook: 45 mins   **prep: 20 mins**   **serves 4**

The small towns Crécy-la-Chapelle and Crécy-en-Ponthieu both lay claim to being the originators of this classic soup and the puréed carrot garnish of the same name.

NUTRITIONAL INFORMATION	
Calories	208
Protein	1g
Carbohydrate	12g
Sugars	6g
Fat	18g
Saturates	12g

INGREDIENTS

8 oz/225 g carrots

6 tbsp butter

2 shallots, finely chopped

pinch of sugar

salt and pepper

⅛ cup long-grain rice

1 fresh thyme sprig

generous 2¾ cups Vegetable Stock (see page 13)

crusty bread, to serve

GARNISH

1 tbsp chopped fresh parsley

Croutons (see page 18)

1   Slice the carrots. Melt 4 tablespoons of the butter in a heavy-bottomed pan. Add the shallots, carrots, sugar, and a pinch of salt, then cover and cook over very low heat, stirring occasionally, for 10 minutes. Stir in the rice and thyme and pour in the Stock. Bring to a boil, then reduce the heat and simmer for 30 minutes.

2   Remove the pan from the heat and let cool slightly. Remove and discard the thyme sprig and pour the soup into a blender or food processor. Process into a smooth paste.

3   Return to a clean pan and re-heat gently. Season to taste with salt and pepper and gradually whisk in the remaining butter in small pieces. Ladle into warmed soup bowls, then garnish with parsley and Croutons and serve immediately.

cook's tip

If you are a meat-eater and you want to add an extra dimension of flavor to the soup, substitute chicken stock for the vegetable stock.

borscht

cook: 1 hr 15 mins   **prep: 30 mins**   **serves 6**

NUTRITIONAL INFORMATION

Calories 169

Protein 3g

Carbohydrate 13g

Sugars 12g

Fat 12g

Saturates 8g

Antonin Carême, chef to Czar Alexander I, is credited with introducing this traditional Russian beet soup to France and so to the rest of Europe. This is a lighter, easier version of his rather elaborate recipe and is suitable for vegetarians. Its strong color make it ideal as an appetizer for a dinner party.

variation

For a more substantial soup, add 2 diced potatoes with the cabbage in Step 3. Cook for an additional 10 minutes, then add the grated beet.

INGREDIENTS

1 onion	1 tbsp white wine vinegar
¼ cup butter	1 tbsp sugar
12 oz/350 g raw beets,	2 large fresh dill sprigs
cut into thin sticks, and	salt and pepper
1 raw beet, grated	4 oz/115 g white cabbage, shredded
1 carrot, cut into thin sticks	⅔ cup sour cream, to garnish
3 celery stalks, thinly sliced	rye bread, to serve (optional)
2 tomatoes, peeled,	
seeded and chopped	
6¼ cups Vegetable Stock	
(see page 13)	

cook's tip

It is not essential to add extra grated beet towards the end of cooking, but this helps to provide the spectacular purple color of the soup and also freshens the flavor.

1 Slice the onion into rings. Melt the butter in a large, heavy-bottomed pan. Add the onion and cook over low heat, stirring occasionally, for 3–5 minutes, or until softened. Add the sticks of beet, carrot, celery, and chopped tomatoes and cook, stirring frequently, for 4–5 minutes.

2 Add the Stock, vinegar, and sugar and snip a tablespoon of dill into the pan. Season to taste with salt and pepper. Bring to a boil, reduce the heat and simmer for 35–40 minutes, or until the vegetables are tender.

3 Stir in the cabbage, cover, and simmer for

10 minutes, then stir in the grated beet, with any juices, and cook for an additional 10 minutes. Ladle the borscht into warmed bowls. Garnish with sour cream and another tablespoon of snipped dill and serve with rye bread.

chinese vegetable soup

serves 4   **prep: 20 mins** ⟲   **cook: 10 mins** ⟳

This deliciously fresh vegetable broth would make an unusual first course for a dinner party or a tasty light lunch. Its Asian ingredients lend an Eastern flavor to the marinated bean curd. The soup is suitable for both vegetarians and vegans.

INGREDIENTS

4 oz/115 g Napa cabbage

2 tbsp peanut oil

8 oz/225 g marinated bean curd, cut into ½-inch/1-cm cubes

2 garlic cloves, thinly sliced

4 scallions, thinly sliced diagonally

1 carrot, thinly sliced

4 cups Vegetable Stock (see page 13)

1 tbsp Chinese rice wine

2 tbsp light soy sauce

1 tsp sugar

salt and pepper

NUTRITIONAL INFORMATION

Calories 117

Protein 6g

Carbohydrate 5g

Sugars 3g

Fat 8g

Saturates 1g

---

variation

If you are unable to find Chinese rice wine, substitute dry sherry. You can also use firm lettuce leaves, such as Boston or romaine, instead of Napa cabbage.

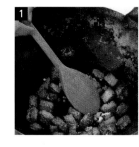

cook's tip

Always use a very sharp knife when cutting tofu because it is soft and easily squashed. A blunt knife will produce unevenly shaped cubes.

1 Shred the Napa cabbage and reserve. Heat the peanut oil in a large preheated wok or skillet. Add the bean curd cubes and stir-fry for 4–5 minutes, or until browned, then remove from the wok with a perforated spoon. Drain on paper towels.

2 Add the garlic, scallions, and carrot to the wok and stir-fry for 2 minutes. Pour in the Stock, Chinese rice wine, and soy sauce, then add the sugar and shredded Napa cabbage. Cook over medium heat for 1–2 minutes, or until heated through.

3 Season to taste with salt and pepper and add the tofu. Ladle the soup into warmed bowls and serve.

gazpacho

serves 6

prep: 30 mins, ↺ **plus 4–8 hrs chilling**

cook: 0 mins ⏱

Andalusia's world famous, chilled vegetable soup is the perfect choice for alfresco entertaining, not least because of its ease of preparation—it involves absolutely no cooking. The soup is suitable for both vegetarians and vegans.

INGREDIENTS

8 oz/225 g fresh white bread

1 cucumber

3 garlic cloves, chopped

1 lb 8 oz/675 g tomatoes, peeled and chopped

2 red bell peppers, seeded and chopped

5 tbsp extra virgin olive oil

5 tbsp white wine vinegar

salt and pepper

scant 3½ cups water

ice cubes, to serve

GARNISH

Croutons (see page 18)

thinly sliced spring onions

peeled and diced cucumber

diced yellow pepper

pitted black olives

NUTRITIONAL INFORMATION

Calories	207
Protein	. . . . .5g
Carbohydrate	. . . . .25g
Sugars	. . . . .7g
Fat	. . . . .10g
Saturates	. . . . .2g

variation

You can vary the ingredients depending on what fresh vegetables are available. Try red onion, scallions, celery, and even avocados.

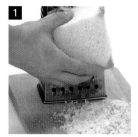

cook's tip

If the soup seems too thick after chilling in the refrigerator in Step 3, you can add a little more water until the consistency is thinner.

1 Grate the bread to make breadcrumbs. Peel, seed, and chop the cucumber. Put them in a bowl with the garlic, tomatoes, bell peppers, oil, and vinegar. Season to taste and mix.

2 Ladle batches of the vegetable mixture into a blender or food processor, adding a little of the water each time, and process until smooth. Transfer the mixture to a bowl.

3 Cover with plastic wrap and chill in the refrigerator for 4–8 hours. To serve, add the ice cubes. Arrange the garnishes in individual dishes and serve with the soup.

vichyssoise

serves 6　　　　**prep: 40 mins, plus 4–8 hrs chilling**　　　　**cook: 35 mins**

Although created by a French chef, this famous chilled leek and potato soup originated in New York, not France. Rich and creamy, it would make a substantial appetizer or lunchtime dish.

INGREDIENTS

1 lb/450 g leeks, white parts only

1 lb/450 g potatoes

¼ cup butter

5 cups water

salt and pepper

2½ cups milk

1¼ cups sour cream

GARNISH

sour cream

2 tbsp snipped fresh chives

NUTRITIONAL INFORMATION

Calories 310

Protein 8g

Carbohydrate 22g

Sugars 9g

Fat 22g

Saturates 14g

 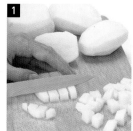 

cook's tip

To make the soup traditionally and for meat-eaters, use chicken stock instead of water.

1 Thinly slice the leeks and cube the potatoes. Melt the butter in a large, heavy-bottomed pan. Add the leeks, cover, and cook over very low heat, stirring occasionally, for 10 minutes.

2 Stir in the potatoes and cook over medium heat, stirring frequently, for 2 minutes.

3 Pour in the water and add a pinch of salt. Bring to a boil, reduce the heat, and simmer for 15–20 minutes, or until the potatoes are tender. Remove the pan from the heat and leave to cool slightly. Ladle into a food processor and process into a paste. Push the mixture through a strainer into a clean pan with a wooden spoon, then stir in the milk. Season to taste, and stir in half of the sour cream.

4 Re-heat the soup. Push through a strainer into a bowl. Stir in the remaining cream, cover with plastic wrap, and let cool. Chill in the refrigerator for 4–8 hours. Serve in chilled bowls, with cream and chives to garnish.

frijoles

cook: 2 hrs   **prep: 15 mins**   **serves 6**

Beans take a starring role in both Mexican cuisine and vegetarian diets. They are a rich source of soluble fiber, and help to reduce cholesterol levels. This dish is suitable for vegetarians and vegans.

NUTRITIONAL INFORMATION

Calories	213
Protein	14g
Carbohydrate	31g
Sugars	5g
Fat	5g
Saturates	1g

INGREDIENTS

2 fresh green chiles

2 cups dried red kidney beans, soaked in cold water for 3 hours

2 onions, chopped

2 garlic cloves, chopped

1 bay leaf

2 tbsp corn oil

salt

2 tomatoes, peeled, seeded and chopped

cook's tip

Some dried pulses, including red kidney beans, contain a toxin that is destroyed only by cooking. It is essential to boil the beans vigorously for 15 minutes, before simmering to finish cooking.

1 Chop the chiles. Drain the beans and place in a pan. Add enough water to cover by 1 inch/2.5 cm. Add half the onion, half the garlic, the chiles, and the bay leaf. Bring to a boil, boil vigorously for 15 minutes, then reduce the heat and simmer for 30 minutes, adding more boiling water if the mixture begins to dry out.

2 Add 1 tablespoon of the oil and simmer for an additional 30 minutes, adding more boiling water if necessary. Season to taste with salt and simmer for an additional 30 minutes, but do not add any more water.

3 Meanwhile, heat the remaining oil in a skillet. Add the remaining onion and garlic and cook, stirring occasionally, for 5 minutes, or until softened. Stir in the chopped tomatoes and cook for an additional 5 minutes. Add 3 tablespoons of the cooked beans to the tomato mixture, mash thoroughly into a paste, then stir the paste into the beans. Heat through gently, then serve.

stuffed mushrooms

cook: 40 minutes   **prep: 20 minutes**   **serves 4**

variation

Meat-eaters could substitute 2 oz/55 g of chopped, fried bacon, 2 oz/55 g of fresh bread crumbs and 2 oz/55 g of ground almonds for the spinach.

A combination of spinach and cheese makes a tasty filling for mushroom caps in this attractive, warm appetizer. The spinach is high in folic acid and vitamin C, and the mushrooms provide substantial amounts of iron, potassium, and vitamin B.

INGREDIENTS

2 oz/55 g feta cheese

12 large mushrooms

3 tbsp dry white wine

3 tbsp water

1 shallot, chopped

1 fresh thyme sprig, finely chopped

2 tsp lemon juice

1 tbsp butter

salt and pepper

2 tsp olive oil

1 garlic clove, finely chopped

6 oz/175 g fresh spinach, coarse stems removed and leaves chopped

cook's tip

There is no need to peel mushrooms unless their skin is leathery or discolored. Just carefully wipe off the dirt with damp kitchen paper.

1 Preheat the oven to 350°F/180°C. Crumble the feta and reserve. Remove the stems from the mushrooms and chop the stems finely.

2 Pour the wine and water into a wide pan and add half the shallot and thyme. Bring to a boil and simmer for 2 minutes. Add the mushroom caps, smooth side down, and sprinkle over the lemon juice. Cover, simmer for 6 minutes, then remove the mushrooms and place on a plate to drain. Return the liquid to a boil, add the mushroom stems and butter, and season with salt. Cook for 6 minutes, or until the liquid has been absorbed. Transfer the stems to a bowl.

3 Heat the olive oil in a clean pan. Add the remaining shallot, the garlic and spinach, and sprinkle with a little salt. Cook over medium heat, stirring, for about 3 minutes, or until all the liquid has evaporated. Stir the spinach mixture into the mushroom stems, season to taste with pepper, then gently stir in the reserved feta.

4 Divide the spinach mixture between the mushroom caps. Place them in a single layer in an ovenproof dish and bake in the preheated oven for 15–20 minutes, or until golden. Serve warm.

serves 4

**prep: 25 mins,
plus 24 hrs marinating**

cook: 25 mins

This mouthwatering selection of Italian marinated vegetables is the perfect choice for an alfresco meal on a warm summer's evening. This dish is suitable for vegetarians and vegans.

INGREDIENTS

1 lb/450 g large mushrooms	3 red bell peppers
5 garlic cloves	3 orange bell peppers
about 2½ cups extra virgin olive oil	4 tbsp fresh basil leaves
1 tbsp finely chopped	pinch of chili powder
fresh rosemary	grated rind of 1 lemon
scant 1 cup dry white wine	8 oz/225 g black olives
salt and pepper	2 tbsp chopped fresh parsley

NUTRITIONAL INFORMATION

Calories	1144
Protein	.5g
Carbohydrate	12g
Sugars	11g
Fat	116g
Saturates	.16g

variation

To make this dish into a meal, you could also serve artichoke hearts, raw vegetables, and dips. If you eat meat, add some sliced ham, tuna, or sardines.

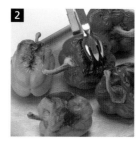

cook's tip

Plan to make these antipasti a day before you will need them. This way, you can leave the dishes to marinate in the refrigerator overnight.

1 Slice the mushrooms and chop 1 garlic clove. Heat 4 tablespoons of the oil in a small pan. Add the chopped garlic and rosemary, pour in the wine and bring to a boil. Reduce the heat, simmer for 3 minutes, then season. Place the mushrooms in a large serving dish and pour the wine mixture over them. Let cool, stirring occasionally, then cover with clingfilm and let marinate in the refrigerator for 8 hours.

2 Meanwhile, cook the bell peppers under a preheated medium–hot broiler, turning frequently, until the skins are blackened. Transfer to a bowl, cover, and let cool, then peel, halve, and seed. Cut the flesh into strips. Place in a clean serving dish. Slice the remaining garlic and add to the dish with the basil. Season with salt, add enough oil to cover, and toss lightly. Cover with plastic wrap and let marinate in the refrigerator for 8 hours.

3 Meanwhile, heat ½ cup of the remaining oil in a pan. Add the chili powder and lemon rind and cook over low heat, stirring, for 2 minutes. Add the olives and cook for 1 minute. Transfer to a clean serving dish, sprinkle with the parsley, and let cool. Cover and let marinate in the refrigerator for 8 hours. Remove the dishes of antipasti from the refrigerator 1 hour before serving.

mushroom bites with garlic mayonnaise

serves 4　　　　**prep: 25 mins**　　　　**cook: 15 mins**

These crispy morsels make delicious canapés and are wonderful warm snacks to serve at parties. They are simple to make, and the mayonnaise can also be used as a dip for raw vegetables.

INGREDIENTS

4 oz/115 g fresh white bread

2 tbsp freshly grated Parmesan cheese

1 tsp paprika

2 egg whites

8 oz/225 g white mushrooms

GARLIC MAYONNAISE

4 garlic cloves, crushed

salt and pepper

2 egg yolks

scant 1 cup extra virgin olive oil

NUTRITIONAL INFORMATION

Calories	.504
Protein	.8g
Carbohydrate	.15g
Sugars	.1g
Fat	.46g
Saturates	.8g

variation

For a herb cream dip, mix 4 tablespoons of chopped herbs with ¾ cup sour cream, 1 chopped garlic clove, lemon juice, and seasoning to taste.

1 Preheat the oven to 375°F/190°C. To make the garlic mayonnaise, put the garlic in a bowl, add a pinch of salt, and mash with the back of a spoon. Add the egg yolks and beat with an electric whisk for 30 seconds, or until creamy. Start beating in the oil, one drop at a time. As the mixture begins to thicken, add the oil in a steady stream, beating constantly. Season to taste with salt and pepper, cover the bowl with plastic wrap, and chill in the refrigerator until required.

2 Line a large cookie sheet with parchment paper. Grate the bread into bread crumbs and place them in a bowl with the Parmesan cheese and paprika. Lightly beat the egg whites in a separate clean bowl, then dip each mushroom first into the egg whites, then into the bread crumbs, and place on the prepared cookie sheet.

3 Bake in the preheated oven for 15 minutes, or until the coating is crisp and golden. Serve immediately with the garlic mayonnaise.

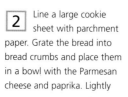

hummus with crudités

cook: 0 mins　　　　**prep: 20 mins**　　　　**serves 4**

Making your own hummus couldn't be simpler and it tastes much better than any shop-bought varieties. This dish is suitable for both vegetarians and vegans.

NUTRITIONAL INFORMATION	
Calories	.311
Protein	11g
Carbohydrate	16g
Sugars	8g
Fat	23g
Saturates	3g

INGREDIENTS

6 oz/175 g canned chickpeas

½ cup sesame seed paste

2 garlic cloves

½ cup lemon juice

salt

2–3 tbsp water

1 tbsp olive oil

1 tbsp chopped fresh parsley

pinch of cayenne pepper

CRUDITES

selection of vegetables, including carrots, cauliflower, and celery

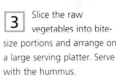

cook's tip

If you don't have a blender or food processor, simply mash the ingredients vigorously in a bowl until smooth and combined, adding enough water to achieve the desired creamy consistency.

1 Drain and rinse the chickpeas. Place them in a blender or food processor with the sesame seed paste, garlic, and lemon juice. Season to taste with salt. Process, gradually adding the water, until smooth and creamy.

2 Scrape the chickpea mixture into a serving bowl and make a hollow in the center. Pour the olive oil into the hollow and sprinkle with the chopped fresh parsley and the cayenne.

3 Slice the raw vegetables into bite-size portions and arrange on a large serving platter. Serve with the hummus.

bean curd tempura

serves 4   **prep: 15 mins** ⟲   **cook: 20 mins** ⟲

Crispy coated vegetables and bean curd accompanied by a sweet, spicy dip give a real taste of Asia in this Japanese-style dish. Bean curd, made from soybeans, is a rich source of protein and calcium, making it a valuable part of the vegetarian diet.

INGREDIENTS

4½ oz/125 g baby zucchini
4½ oz/125 g baby carrots
4½ oz/125 g baby corn cobs
4½ oz/125 g baby leeks
2 baby eggplants
8 oz/225 g firm bean curd
(drained weight)
vegetable oil, for deep-frying
julienne strips of carrot,
fresh gingerroot and baby
leek, to garnish
freshly cooked noodles, to serve

BATTER

2 egg yolks
1¼ cups water
generous 1½ cups all-purpose flour

DIPPING SAUCE

5 tbsp mirin
5 tbsp Japanese soy sauce
2 tsp clear honey
1 garlic clove, crushed
1 tsp grated fresh gingerroot

NUTRITIONAL INFORMATION

Calories 582

Protein 16g

Carbohydrate 65g

Sugars 10g

Fat 27g

Saturates 4g

---

variation

If you are unable to find mirin, you can substitute dry sherry. You can also use other vegetables such as broccoli and cauliflower for the tempura.

cook's tip

The bean curd and vegetables will be too hot to eat immediately after deep-frying, so make the dipping sauce after cooking, as suggested in Step 6. This lets the tempura cool before serving.

1 Slice the zucchini and carrots in half lengthwise. Trim the corn and trim the leeks at both ends. Cut the eggplants into fourths and cut the bean curd into 1-inch/2.5-cm wide batons.

2 To make the batter, mix the egg yolks and water together in a large bowl. Strain 1¼ cups of the flour and

whisk with a balloon whisk to form a thick batter. Don't worry if there are any lumps. Heat the oil for deep-frying to 350–375°F/180–190°C, or until a cube of bread browns in 30 seconds.

3 Place the remaining flour on a large plate. Toss the baby vegetables and bean curd in the flour to coat.

4 Dip the bean curd in the batter and deep-fry for 2–3 minutes, or until lightly golden brown. Drain on paper towels and keep warm.

5 Dip the vegetables in the batter and deep-fry, a few at a time, for 3–4 minutes, or until golden brown. Drain and place on a warmed serving plate.

6 To make the dipping sauce, mix all the ingredients together in a bowl, then transfer to a serving dish. Serve with the vegetables and bean curd, accompanied with noodles and garnished with the julienne vegetables.

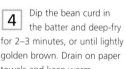

fiery salsa

cook: 0 mins　　　　**prep: 30 mins**　　　　**serves 4**

NUTRITIONAL INFORMATION

Calories 328

Protein 4g

Carbohydrate 21g

Sugars 2g

Fat 26g

Saturates 5g

Make this delicious Mexican-style salsa to perk up jaded palates. Its lively flavors really get the taste buds going, but if you prefer the salsa slightly milder, just use one fresh chile. Serve with plenty of warmed tortilla chips.

INGREDIENTS

3 small fresh red chiles

1 tbsp lime or lemon juice

2 large ripe avocados

2-inch/5-cm piece cucumber

2 tomatoes, peeled

1 small garlic clove, crushed

few drops of Tabasco sauce

salt and pepper

lime or lemon slices, to garnish

warmed tortilla chips, to serve

variation

Serve with toasted pita bread, cut into strips, or a selection of raw vegetables such as carrot and cucumber batons, instead of the tortilla chips.

cook's tip

Try to find very ripe avocados for this salsa as underripe ones will be difficult to mash. Adding lime juice to the salsa helps prevent the avocado turning brown, but do not let it stand for too long.

1 To make chile "flowers" for the garnish, slice a chile from stalk to tip several times without removing the stalk. Place in a bowl of iced water until the "petals" open out. Repeat.

2 Remove and discard the stem and seeds from the remaining chile. Chop the flesh finely and put in a bowl.

3 Add the lime or lemon juice to the bowl. Halve, pit, and peel the avocados. Add the flesh to the bowl and mash thoroughly with a fork. The salsa should be slightly chunky.

4 Chop the cucumber and tomatoes finely and add to the avocado mixture with the crushed garlic.

5 Stir in the Tabasco sauce and season to taste with salt and pepper. Transfer the dip to a serving bowl. Garnish with lime slices and the chile flowers.

6 Place the bowl on a large plate, surround with warmed tortilla chips, and serve immediately.

stuffed vine leaves

These refreshing little parcels with their fragrant, flavored rice filling are a lovely way to start a summer meal. Serve these Mediterranean morsels warm, the way the Greeks do. This dish is suitable for both vegetarians and vegans.

INGREDIENTS

1 bunch of fresh mint	1¼ cups boiling Vegetable
1 bunch of fresh parsley	Stock (see page 13)
8 oz/225 g fresh vine leaves	strips of lemon rind, to garnish
4 scallions, finely chopped	
2 shallots, finely chopped	DRESSING
¼ cup slivered almonds, toasted	½ cup extra virgin olive oil
finely grated rind of 1 lemon	salt and pepper
scant 1 cup long-grain rice	3 tbsp lemon juice
½ cup olive oil	1 tbsp chopped fresh mint
salt	

NUTRITIONAL INFORMATION

Calories	.407
Protein	.5g
Carbohydrate	.27g
Sugars	.1g
Fat	.32g
Saturates	.4g

variation

If you can't find fresh vine leaves, use preserved leaves, which do not need blanching. Rinse thoroughly and pat dry before cutting off the stems.

cook's tip

It is important to use long-grain rice for this dish to make sure that the stuffing is not too sticky, otherwise it will be difficult to handle. The rice grains should remain separate when cooked.

1 Chop enough fresh mint and parsley to fill 6 tablespoons. Blanch the vine leaves in boiling water for 5 minutes, then refresh under cold running water and pat dry. Cut off the stems.

2 Mix the scallions, shallots, almonds, parsley, mint, lemon rind, and rice in a bowl and add half the oil. Season with salt. Spread out a vine leaf on a counter and place a spoonful of the filling near the stem end. Fold the stem end over, fold the sides in, and roll up to make a parcel. Repeat with the remaining leaves and filling.

3 Line the bottom of a large pan with any remaining vine leaves and place the parcels on top in a single layer. Sprinkle with the remaining oil and pour in the Stock. Place a plate on top of the leaves to keep them submerged, then cover the pan and simmer for 45 minutes. To make the dressing, pour the oil into a small serving bowl and season well with salt and pepper. Whisk in the lemon juice and stir in the mint. Transfer the vine leaves to a serving dish, garnish with strips of lemon rind, and serve, warm or cold, with the dressing.

celery root rémoulade

serves 4   **prep: 10 mins** ⟳   **cook: 0 mins** ⟳

Celery root served with a rémoulade sauce—a mustard-flavored mayonnaise—is a classically simple French dish, ideal served as an appetizer or as a side dish to a main meal.

INGREDIENTS

scant 1 cup Mayonnaise
(see page 13)
2 tsp lemon juice
1 tbsp Dijon mustard
salt and pepper
8 oz/225 g celery root
1 shallot
6 lettuce leaves
snipped fresh chives, to garnish

NUTRITIONAL INFORMATION

Calories 236

Protein 3g

Carbohydrate 4g

Sugars 3g

Fat 24g

Saturates 3g

1 Mix the Mayonnaise, lemon juice, and mustard together in a large bowl and season to taste. Peel and grate the celery root into the mixture.

2 Grate the shallot and stir it in thoroughly, making sure the celery root is well coated in the dressing.

3 Line a salad bowl with the lettuce leaves and spoon the celery root mixture into the center. Sprinkle with the chives and serve.

cook's tip

You may need to cut the celery root into large chunks to make it easier to grate. Do not grate it in advance, as it will discolor quickly when exposed to the air.

imam bayildi

cook: 45 mins **prep: 15 mins, plus 2 hrs** **serves 4**
salting, cooling, and chilling

*The name of this dish means "the Imam fainted." A Muslim holy
man was said to have been so overjoyed by its aroma that he
swooned with delight. It is suitable for vegetarians and vegans.*

NUTRITIONAL INFORMATION

Calories 207

Protein 3g

Carbohydrate 23g

Sugars 21g

Fat 12g

Saturates 2g

INGREDIENTS

2 eggplants

salt and pepper

4 tbsp olive oil

2 onions, thinly sliced

2 garlic cloves, finely chopped

1 green bell pepper, seeded and sliced

14 oz/400 g canned chopped tomatoes

3 tbsp sugar

1 tsp ground coriander

2 tbsp chopped fresh cilantro

cook's tip

Even after salting, eggplants
tend to absorb a lot of oil, so
you may need to add a little
more before cooking the
onions in Step 2.

1 Preheat the oven
to 375°F/190°C. Halve
the eggplants lengthwise, slash
the flesh 4 or 5 times, and
sprinkle generously with salt.
Place in a colander and set
aside for 30 minutes. Rinse
and pat dry.

2 Heat the olive oil in a
large, heavy-bottomed
skillet, then add the eggplants,

cut side down, and cook for
5 minutes. Drain well on
paper towels and place in a
casserole. Add the onions,
garlic, and green bell pepper
to the skillet, and cook, stirring
occasionally, for 10 minutes.
Stir in the tomatoes, sugar,
and ground coriander and
season to taste with salt and
pepper, then stir in the
chopped fresh cilantro.

3 Spoon the onion and
tomato mixture on top
of the eggplant halves, cover,
and bake in the preheated
oven for 30 minutes. Remove
from the oven and let cool.
Chill in the refrigerator for
1 hour before serving.

pakoras

cook: 15 mins   **prep: 10 mins**   **serves 6**

variation

You could also serve these Indian fritters with store-bought mango chutney, for a slightly sweeter dish.

These flavorsome Indian fritters can be made with many different vegetables. Eggplants are the most popular, because they provide a succulent center inside the spicy batter coating.

INGREDIENTS

2 small eggplants	**TOMATO CHUTNEY**
9 oz/250 g besan flour	1 red bell pepper, seeded and chopped
1 tsp ground cumin	4 tomatoes, chopped
1 tsp ground coriander	2 fresh green chiles, seeded
1 tsp paprika	1 garlic clove, chopped
salt	3 tbsp tomato paste
½ tsp dried thyme	1 tbsp chopped fresh cilantro
1 tsp black onion seeds	1 tsp chili powder
2 tbsp lukewarm water	pinch of salt
peanut or corn oil,	pinch of sugar
for deep-frying	

cook's tip

Besan flour, made from ground chickpeas, is available from specialist Indian food stores. It is now also stocked by some major food stores and by health food stores.

1 To make the tomato chutney, place all of the ingredients in a blender or food processor. Process until fairly smooth, then transfer into a bowl and let chill in the refrigerator.

2 Trim the eggplants, slice them thickly, and reserve. Sift the flour, cumin, coriander, paprika, and a pinch of salt into a large mixing bowl and stir in the thyme and onion seeds. Gradually add the lukewarm water and mix to make a smooth batter.

3 Heat the oil in a deep-fryer or large pan to 350–375°F/180–190°C, or until a teaspoon of batter dropped into the oil rises immediately to the surface.

4 Dip the eggplant slices in the batter, a few at a time, and drop into the oil. Cook for 3–4 minutes, or until crisp and golden brown. Remove with a perforated spoon and drain on paper towels. Keep warm while you cook the remainder. Serve hot with the tomato chutney.

caponata

serves 4   **prep: 10 mins** ⏲   **cook: 25 mins** ⏲

This is a Sicilian speciality, which varies slightly from one part of the island to the other, but it always contains eggplant, onion, celery, tomato, and capers. It is traditionally served at room temperature. This dish is suitable for both vegetarians and vegans.

INGREDIENTS

4 tbsp olive oil	1 tbsp sugar
1 onion, sliced	12 black olives, pitted
2 celery stalks, sliced	2 tbsp capers
1 eggplant, diced	salt
5 plum tomatoes, chopped	3 tbsp chopped fresh flatleaf parsley,
1 garlic clove, finely chopped	to garnish
3 tbsp red wine vinegar	

NUTRITIONAL INFORMATION

Calories 178

Protein 2g

Carbohydrate 12g

Sugars 11g

Fat 14g

Saturates. 2g

---

variation

If you are not cooking for vegetarians, add 4 anchovies with the capers in Step 3. Desalt them by soaking in a little milk for 5 minutes before using.

cook's tip

Caponata tastes best if you make it a little while ahead of serving it. This gives the strong flavors of this traditional soup plenty of time to develop and blend before it is served.

1 Heat 2 tablespoons of the olive oil in a large, heavy-bottomed pan. Add the onion and celery and cook over low heat, stirring frequently, for 5 minutes, or until softened. Add the remaining oil with the eggplant and cook, stirring constantly, for 10 minutes.

2 Stir in the tomatoes, garlic, vinegar, and sugar. Cover the surface with a circle of waxed paper and simmer for 10 minutes.

3 Stir in the olives and capers and season to taste with salt. Transfer the mixture to a serving dish and

let cool to room temperature. Sprinkle with the chopped parsley and serve.

snacks & light meals

It's a busy weekend, there isn't much time for cooking lunch, and a heavy meal would slow you down, but you need to boost your reserves of energy—look no further, because this chapter has the perfect solution. Light, easily digested, and packed with flavor, vegetable dishes are ideal for just such contingencies.

There are recipes for all kinds of vegetables, from potatoes—try the classic curry Aloo Gobi (see page 63)—to eggplants—a delicious topping on Pizza alla Siciliana (see page 83). Vegetables are marvelously versatile and combine superbly with each other, as in Ratatouille (see page 66) and with a wide range of other ingredients, from eggs and cheese to pasta and pastry. This chapter includes many family favorites, often with a new twist, such as Cauliflower Cheese Surprise (see page 72), and also features some recipes that will coax even the fussiest child to eat up their greens. Quick and easy dishes include Summer Stir-Fry (see page 71) and Spanish Omelet (see page 93), while the more time-consuming Leek & Onion Tartlets (see page 80) or Lattice Pie (see page 77) would look wonderful on a party buffet table.

Hot or cold, simple or sophisticated, robust or subtle, plain or fancy, there is sure to be a recipe that fits the bill, whether you are cooking a late evening snack for a house full of teenagers, creating a family lunch, or preparing picnic fare.

paprika potatoes

⏱ **cook: 1 hr 10 mins**   ⏲ **prep: 15 mins**   **serves 4**

NUTRITIONAL INFORMATION

Calories 177

Protein 6g

Carbohydrate 38g

Sugars 4g

Fat 1g

Saturates 0g

variation

To make a richer dish with an extra hint of flavor, substitute sour cream for the plain yogurt in Steps 2 and 3.

Baked potatoes are an easy and welcome snack on a cold day, and here they are given a new twist with an interesting, colorful, creamy filling livened up with a hint of garlic.

INGREDIENTS

4 baking potatoes

½ cup Vegetable Stock (see page 13)

1 onion, finely chopped

1 garlic clove, finely chopped

½ cup plain yogurt

2 tsp paprika

salt and pepper

cook's tip

If you like to eat the nutritious skin of baked potatoes, to keep it crisp, rub the potatoes with a little olive oil before putting them in the oven.

1 Preheat the oven to 400°F/200°C. Prick the potatoes with a fork and bake for 1 hour, or until tender. Just before the potatoes are ready, pour the Vegetable Stock into a pan and add the chopped onion and garlic. Bring to a boil and simmer for 5 minutes.

2 Remove the potatoes from the oven and cut a slice from the top of each, lengthwise. Do not switch off the oven. Carefully scoop out the flesh with a teaspoon, leaving the shells. Stir the flesh into the onions, add half the yogurt and 1½ teaspoons of the paprika, season, and stir. Push through a strainer with the back of a wooden spoon.

3 Spoon the potato mixture into the potato shells and return to the oven for 10 minutes, or until heated through. Top the potatoes with the remaining yogurt, sprinkle over the remaining paprika, and serve.

vegetable croquettes

serves 12   **prep: 20 mins**   **cook: 30 mins**

These croquettes, made from a spicy vegetable mixture, are delightfully easy to make and taste delicious. They make a great snack, or can form part of a more substantial meal.

INGREDIENTS

2 large potatoes, sliced	1 tsp ground coriander
1 onion, sliced	pinch of ground turmeric
½ cauliflower, cut into small florets	1 tsp salt
1¾ oz/50 g cooked peas	1 cup fresh white bread crumbs
1 tbsp spinach paste	1¼ cups vegetable oil
2–3 fresh green chiles	
1 tbsp fresh cilantro leaves	TO GARNISH
1 tsp finely chopped fresh gingerroot	fresh chile strips
1 tsp crushed garlic	fresh cilantro sprigs

NUTRITIONAL INFORMATION

Calories 268

Protein 2g

Carbohydrate 9g

Sugars 1g

Fat 25g

Saturates 3g

variation

Serve the croquettes with plain yogurt, Mayonnaise (see page 13), or even Garlic Mayonnaise (see page 40).

cook's tip

If you wish to prepare the croquettes a few hours in advance, place them on a plate and let cool after coating them in bread crumbs in Step 3, then store them in the refrigerator until required.

1 Place the potato and onion slices and the cauliflower florets in a large, heavy-bottomed pan, cover with water, and bring to a boil. Reduce the heat and simmer until the potatoes are cooked through, then remove the vegetables from the pan with a perforated spoon and place in a colander to drain completely. Reserve.

2 Add the peas and spinach paste to the vegetables and mash with a fork. Using a sharp knife, finely chop the chiles and fresh cilantro leaves and mix with the gingerroot, garlic, ground coriander, turmeric, and salt.

3 Blend the spice mixture into the vegetables, mixing with a fork to make a

paste. Place the bread crumbs on a large plate. Break off 10–12 small balls from the spice paste and flatten them with the palm of your hand to make thick, flat circles. Dip each croquette in the bread crumbs, coating well.

4 Heat the vegetable oil in a large, heavy-bottomed skillet and shallow-

fry the croquettes, in batches, until golden brown, turning occasionally. Transfer to serving plates and garnish with chile strips and fresh cilantro sprigs. Serve hot.

oeufs au nid

serves 4   **prep: 15 mins**   **cook: 40 mins**

Soft-baked eggs laying on a bed of soft mashed potato look just as if they are resting in a nest and taste superb. This straightforward dish is very easy to make, but looks impressive.

INGREDIENTS

2 lb/900 g floury potatoes, unpeeled

salt and pepper

¾ cup butter

scant 1 cup milk

4 eggs

2 oz/55 g Cheddar cheese

NUTRITIONAL INFORMATION

Calories	.673
Protein	.18g
Carbohydrate	.42g
Sugars	.4g
Fat	.49g
Saturates	.30g

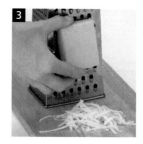

cook's tip

Don't be tempted to beat the cooked potatoes in a food processor, as this will make them sticky and will fail to incorporate enough air to make a light mash.

1 Preheat the oven to 400°F/200°C. Cook the potatoes in lightly salted boiling water for about 25 minutes, or until tender. Drain and peel. Place the potatoes in a bowl with ½ cup of the butter and mash until no lumps remain. Season to taste with salt and pepper. Pour in half the milk and beat vigorously with a whisk.

Continue whisking, adding more milk if necessary, until the potato is light and smooth.

2 Use some of the remaining butter to grease an ovenproof dish. Spoon the mashed potato into the dish and make 4 hollows. Dot a little butter in each of the hollows, crack 1 egg into each hollow, and season.

3 Using the tines of a fork, carefully make grooves around each egg to create a "nest." Grate the cheese and sprinkle it over, then bake in the preheated oven for 15 minutes, or until the egg whites are set, but the yolks are still runny. Serve immediately.

feta & potato cakes

cook: 35 mins   **prep: 20 mins, plus 1 hr chilling**   **serves 4**

Served with a salad, these tasty vegetable patties make a satisfying light lunch and are very easy to prepare, too. The feta cheese gives them a tangy flavor, and is complemented by the scallions.

NUTRITIONAL INFORMATION

Calories 269

Protein 9g

Carbohydrate 24g

Sugars 1g

Fat 16g

Saturates 1g

INGREDIENTS

1 lb 2 oz/500 g floury
potatoes, unpeeled

salt and pepper

4 scallions, chopped

4 oz/115 g feta cheese, crumbled

2 tsp chopped fresh thyme

1 egg, beaten

1 tbsp lemon juice

all-purpose flour, for dusting

3 tbsp corn oil

fresh chives, to garnish

cook's tip

You can substitute other smooth cheeses such as goat cheese for the feta, if you have some in the refrigerator that needs using up.

1 Cook the potatoes in lightly salted boiling water for about 25 minutes, or until tender. Drain and peel. Place the potatoes in a bowl and mash well with a potato masher or fork.

2 Add the scallions, feta, thyme, egg, and lemon juice and season to taste with salt and pepper. Mix thoroughly. Cover the bowl with plastic wrap and chill in the refrigerator for 1 hour.

3 Take small handfuls of the potato mixture and roll into balls about the size of a walnut between the palms of your hands. Flatten each one slightly and dust all over with flour. Heat the oil in a skillet over high heat and cook the potato cakes, in batches, if necessary, until golden brown on both sides. Drain on paper towels and serve, garnished with chives.

aloo gobi

cook: 20 mins **prep: 20 mins** **serves 4**

NUTRITIONAL INFORMATION

Calories	164
Protein	5g
Carbohydrate	22g
Sugars	3g
Fat	7g
Saturates	1g

variation

For a slightly sweeter tang, try substituting fresh red chiles for the green chiles in Step 1.

It is not surprising that this vegetable curry is so popular, as it looks attractive, smells wonderful, and tastes superb. This spicy dish is suitable for both vegetarians and vegans.

INGREDIENTS

1 lb/450 g potatoes, unpeeled

2 tbsp peanut or corn oil

1 tsp cumin seeds

2 fresh green chiles, seeded and finely chopped

1 cauliflower, cut into florets

1 tsp ground cumin

1 tsp ground coriander

½ tsp ground turmeric

¼ tsp chili powder

salt and pepper

chopped fresh cilantro, to garnish

cook's tip

Make sure that you choose a fresh cauliflower with plenty of leaves, which protects the flower inside. The flower itself should be creamy white, with no brown patches.

1 Cut the potatoes into 1-inch/2.5-cm pieces. Cook them in a pan of boiling water for 10 minutes. Meanwhile, heat the oil in a large, heavy-bottomed skillet. Add the cumin seeds and cook, stirring constantly, for 1½ minutes, or until they begin to pop and give off their aroma. Add the chiles and cook, stirring, for 1 minute.

2 Add the cauliflower and cook, stirring constantly, for 5 minutes, then remove from the heat while you drain the potatoes.

3 Add the potatoes, ground cumin, ground coriander, turmeric, and chili powder to the skillet and season to taste with salt and pepper. Return to the heat

and cook, stirring frequently, for 10 minutes, or until all the vegetables are tender. Transfer to a warmed serving dish, garnish with the fresh cilantro and serve.

bubble & squeak

serves 4   **prep: 15 mins**   **cook: 1 hr**

Originally created to use up leftover vegetables from the Sunday roast, bubble and squeak is now a popular dish in its own right. This dish is suitable for vegetarians.

INGREDIENTS

1 lb/450 g potatoes, unpeeled

generous ¼ cup butter

salt and pepper

8 oz/225 g cabbage

2–3 tbsp water

4 tbsp corn oil

1 onion, finely chopped

NUTRITIONAL INFORMATION

Calories 348

Protein 4g

Carbohydrate 26g

Sugars 6g

Fat 26g

Saturates 11g

variation

Try using Brussels sprouts instead of cabbage. Cook in lightly salted boiling water for 3–5 minutes. Drain, chop, and add to the potato in Step 2.

1 Cook the potatoes in lightly salted boiling water for 25 minutes, or until tender. Drain and peel, then cut them into dice. Place the potatoes in a large bowl with all but 2 teaspoons of the butter and mash until no lumps remain. Season to taste with salt and pepper. Meanwhile, shred the cabbage, place it in a large,

heavy-bottomed pan, and add the remaining butter and the water. Cover and cook over low heat, shaking the pan occasionally, for 10 minutes, or until tender.

2 Mix the cabbage and mashed potato together in a bowl and season to taste with salt and pepper. Heat half the oil in a heavy-bottomed

skillet. Add the onion and cook, stirring occasionally, for 5 minutes, or until softened. Add the potato and cabbage mixture and press down with the back of a wooden spoon to make a flat, even cake.

3 Cook over medium heat for 15 minutes, until the underside is golden brown. Invert the vegetable

cake on to a large plate. Add the remaining oil to the skillet. Return the cake to the skillet to cook the other side. Cook for 10 minutes, or until the second side is golden brown. Transfer to a plate, cut into wedges, and serve.

red onion bruschetta

🕐 **cook: 20 mins**   ⏲ **prep: 10 mins**   **serves 4**

Garlic-flavored toast is topped with a melt-in-the-mouth mixture of caramelized onions, olives, and melted goat cheese. This dish makes a wonderful dinner party appetizer.

NUTRITIONAL INFORMATION

Calories 418

Protein 11g

Carbohydrate 42g

Sugars 14g

Fat 24g

Saturates 6g

INGREDIENTS

6 tbsp extra virgin olive oil

4 red onions, thickly sliced

2 tbsp balsamic vinegar

8 black olives, pitted and chopped

1 tsp fresh thyme leaves

4 thick slices of rustic bread,
such as ciabatta

4 garlic cloves

4 oz/115 g goat cheese, sliced

1 Heat 2 tablespoons of the olive oil in a large, heavy-bottomed skillet. Add the onions and cook over low heat, stirring occasionally, for 5 minutes, or until softened. Increase the heat to medium and cook, stirring occasionally, until the onions begin to color. Add the balsamic vinegar and cook, stirring constantly, until it has almost completely evaporated. Stir in the olives and fresh thyme leaves.

2 Meanwhile, toast the bread on 1 side under a preheated hot broiler. Rub the toasted sides with the garlic cloves. Place on the broiler rack, toasted side down, and drizzle with the remaining olive oil. Toast the second side.

3 Divide the onion mixture between the slices of toast and top with the cheese. Place under the broiler for 2 minutes, or until the cheese has melted. Transfer to a large serving plate and serve immediately.

variation

Miniature versions of these delicious toasts make great party snacks. Use a French stick or 2 sfilatini (thin ciabatta) instead of the large ciabatta.

ratatouille

serves 4   **prep: 30 mins**   **cook: 1 hr**

The secret to making a successful ratatouille is to cook the vegetables gently so that they sweat in the oil and their own juices to produce a fabulous mingling of flavors. This dish is suitable for both vegetarians and vegans.

INGREDIENTS

2 eggplants	⅔ cup olive oil
4 zucchini	1 bouquet garni
2 yellow bell peppers	3 large tomatoes, peeled,
2 red bell peppers	seeded and coarsely chopped
2 onions	salt and pepper
2 garlic cloves	

NUTRITIONAL INFORMATION

Calories	.360
Protein	.5g
Carbohydrate	.21g
Sugars	.16g
Fat	.29g
Saturates	.4g

variation

To use fresh herbs instead of the bouquet garni, substitute 1 tablespoon each of chopped basil and parsley and 2 teaspoons of fresh thyme leaves.

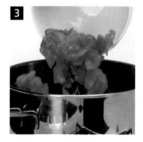

cook's tip

You can buy ready-made bouquet garni, which comes in a bag like a tea bag. If you prefer to use fresh herbs, tie 3 parsley sprigs, 2 thyme sprigs, and a bay leaf together.

1 Roughly chop the eggplants and zucchini, and seed and chop the bell peppers. Slice the onions and finely chop the garlic. Heat the oil in a large pan. Add the onions and cook over low heat, stirring occasionally, for 5 minutes, or until softened. Add the garlic and cook, stirring frequently for an additional 2 minutes.

2 Add the eggplants, zucchini, and bell peppers. Increase the heat to medium and cook, stirring occasionally, until the bell peppers begin to color. Add the bouquet garni, reduce the heat, cover, and simmer gently for 40 minutes.

3 Stir in the chopped tomatoes and season to taste with salt and pepper. Re-cover the pan and simmer gently for an additional 10 minutes. Remove and discard the bouquet garni. Serve warm or cold.

scrambled bean curd

serves 4   prep: 10 mins   cook: 10 mins

This is a delicious dish which would serve equally well as a light lunch or supper. It is quick to prepare, and makes an excellent after-school snack for hungry children.

INGREDIENTS

6 tbsp margarine

1 lb/450 g smoked firm bean curd (drained weight)

1 red onion, chopped

1 red bell pepper, seeded and chopped

4 ciabatta rolls

2 tbsp chopped mixed fresh herbs

salt and pepper

fresh chives, to garnish

NUTRITIONAL INFORMÁTION

Calories	392
Protein	. . . . .16g
Carbohydrate	. . . . .35g
Sugars	. . . . .6g
Fat	. . . . .22g
Saturates	. . . . .4g

cook's tip

Smoked bean curd adds extra flavor to this dish; but marinated bean curd could be used instead. Rub the cut surface of a garlic clove over the toasted ciabatta rolls for extra flavor.

1 Melt the margarine in a skillet and crumble the bean curd into it. Add the onion and bell pepper and cook, stirring occasionally, for 3–4 minutes.

2 Meanwhile, preheat the broiler to medium. Slice the ciabatta rolls in half and toast them under the broiler for 2–3 minutes, turning once, then transfer to a serving plate.

3 Add the chopped herbs to the bean curd and vegetable mixture, stir until well mixed, and season to taste with salt and pepper. Spoon the bean curd mixture on to the toast and garnish with fresh chives. Serve immediately.

garlic mushrooms on toast

cook: 10 mins   prep: 10 mins   serves 4

This dish is so simple to prepare and looks great if you use a variety of mushrooms for shape and texture. Serve the mushrooms on ciabatta or whole-wheat toast, if you prefer.

NUTRITIONAL INFORMATION

Calories 366

Protein 9g

Carbohydrate 45g

Sugars 2g

Fat 18g

Saturates 4g

INGREDIENTS

5½ tbsp margarine

2 garlic cloves, crushed

12 oz/350 g mixed mushrooms, such as open-cap, white, oyster, and shiitake, sliced

8 slices French bread

1 tbsp chopped fresh parsley

salt and pepper

1 Preheat the broiler to medium. Melt the margarine in a large, heavy-bottomed skillet. Add the garlic and cook, stirring constantly, for 30 seconds.

2 Add the mushrooms and cook, turning occasionally, for 5 minutes.

3 Toast the French bread slices under the preheated broiler for 2–3 minutes, turning once. Transfer the toasts to a large serving plate.

4 Toss the parsley into the mushrooms, mixing well, and season to taste with salt and pepper.

5 Spoon the mushroom mixture over the toasted bread slices and serve immediately.

cook's tip

Always store mushrooms for a maximum of 24–36 hours in the refrigerator, in paper bags, as they sweat in plastic. Wild mushrooms should be washed but other varieties can simply be wiped with paper towels.

summer stir-fry

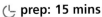

cook: 10 mins   **prep: 15 mins**   **serves 4**

NUTRITIONAL INFORMATION

Calories	105
Protein	5g
Carbohydrate	6g
Sugars	5g
Fat	7g
Saturates	1g

variation

For a more Chinese flavor, add 1 tablespoon dark soy sauce with the vegetables in Step 3, cover the wok or skillet, and steam for 2–3 minutes.

Stir-fries are great when you don't want to spend a lot of time in the kitchen. They are wonderful for vegetables, too, because rapid cooking helps to preserve flavor, color, and texture. This dish is suitable for both vegetarians and vegans.

INGREDIENTS

4 oz/115 g green beans

4 oz/115 g snow peas

4 oz/115 g carrots

4 oz/115 g asparagus spears

½ red bell pepper

½ orange bell pepper

½ yellow bell pepper

2 celery stalks

3 scallions

2 tbsp peanut or corn oil

1 tsp finely chopped fresh gingerroot

2 garlic cloves, finely chopped

4 oz/115 g broccoli florets

salt

Chinese chives, to garnish

cook's tip

Slice fresh vegetables diagonally to maximize their surface area. This makes sure that they will cook more rapidly and evenly.

1 Slice the green beans, snow peas, carrots, asparagus, bell peppers, celery, and scallions and reserve. Heat half the oil in a preheated wok or heavy-bottomed skillet. Add the ginger and garlic and stir-fry for a few seconds, then add the green beans and stir-fry for 2 minutes.

2 Add the snow peas, stir-fry for 1 minute, then add the broccoli florets, carrots, and asparagus and stir-fry for 2 minutes.

3 Add the remaining oil, the bell peppers, celery, and scallions and stir-fry for a further 2–3 minutes, or until all the vegetables are crisp and tender. Season to taste with salt and serve immediately, garnished with Chinese chives.

cauliflower cheese surprise

serves 4   **prep: 15 mins** ⟳   **cook: 20 mins** ♨

The surprise is all the other delicious ingredients cooked with the cauliflower in this version of the well-known family favorite, from onions and mushrooms to tomatoes and corn. These colorful extra ingredients nestle secretly beneath the cauliflower florets and cheese sauce, to be revealed when the dish is served.

NUTRITIONAL INFORMATION

Calories	.549
Protein	.24g
Carbohydrate	.43g
Sugars	.21g
Fat	.32g
Saturates	.17g

INGREDIENTS

2 tbsp corn oil

2 onions, chopped

4 oz/115 g mushrooms, chopped

4 tomatoes, peeled and chopped

7 oz/200 g canned corn
kernels, drained

salt and pepper

1 large cauliflower, cut into florets

2½ cups Cheese Sauce (see page 90),
made with 2½ oz/70 g Cheddar and
2½ oz/70 g Swiss cheese

4 tbsp freshly grated Parmesan cheese

4 tbsp dry bread crumbs

variation

For an attractive effect, use half cauliflower and half broccoli florets for the top layer of this dish.

cook's tip

Remember not to overcook the cauliflower, otherwise it will lose its creamy color and become too soft to handle when you layer it over the other vegetables.

1 Heat the corn oil in a heavy-bottomed skillet. Add the onions and cook over low heat, stirring occasionally, for 5 minutes, or until softened. Add the mushrooms and cook, stirring occasionally, for 5 minutes. Add the tomatoes and corn kernels, season to taste with salt and pepper, mix well, and heat through.

2 Meanwhile, cook the cauliflower florets in a large, heavy-bottomed pan of lightly salted boiling water for 5–10 minutes, or until just tender. Drain and keep warm.

3 Stir ⅔ cup of the Cheese Sauce into the onion, mushroom, and corn mixture, then spoon the mixture into a large, flameproof dish. Top with the cauliflower and pour the remaining Cheese Sauce over it. Mix the Parmesan cheese and bread crumbs together, then sprinkle them over the top. Place under a preheated hot broiler for 3–5 minutes, or until lightly browned. Serve.

bean curd skewers

Bean curd is full of protein, vitamins, and minerals and it develops a fabulous flavor when marinated in garlic and herbs. These skewers can be cooked on a barbecue grill or under the broiler.

INGREDIENTS

12 oz/350 g firm bean curd
(drained weight)
1 red bell pepper
1 yellow bell pepper
2 zucchini
8 white mushrooms
lemon slices, to garnish

MARINADE

grated rind and juice of ½ lemon
1 garlic clove, crushed
½ tsp chopped fresh rosemary
½ tsp chopped fresh thyme
1 tbsp walnut oil

NUTRITIONAL INFORMATION

Calories	.149
Protein	.13g
Carbohydrate	.5g
Sugars	.5g
Fat	.9g
Saturates	.1g

cook's tip

If using wooden skewers, remember to soak them in a bowl of cold water for 30 minutes before using to prevent them burning on the broiler or barbecue grill.

1 Preheat the barbecue grill. To make the marinade, mix the lemon rind and juice, garlic, rosemary, thyme, and oil together in a shallow dish.

2 Drain the bean curd, pat dry on paper towels, and cut it into squares with a sharp knife.

Add to the marinade and toss to coat thoroughly. Let the bean curd marinate for 20–30 minutes.

3 Meanwhile, seed the bell peppers and cut the flesh into 1-inch/2.5-cm pieces. Blanch in a pan of boiling water for 4 minutes, refresh in cold water, and drain.

4 Using a canelle knife or swivel vegetable peeler, remove strips of peel from the zucchini. Cut the zucchini into 1-inch/2.5-cm chunks.

5 Remove the bean curd from the marinade, reserving the marinade. Thread the bean curd on to 8 wooden skewers, alternating with the

bell peppers, zucchini, and white mushrooms.

6 Grill the skewers over medium hot coals for 6 minutes, turning and basting with the reserved marinade.

7 Transfer the skewers to serving plates, garnish with lemon slices, and serve.

spring rolls

cook: 30–35 mins

prep: 20 mins, plus 25 mins soaking

serves 12

Thin slices of vegetables are wrapped in dough and deep-fried until crisp. Spring roll wrappers are available fresh or frozen.

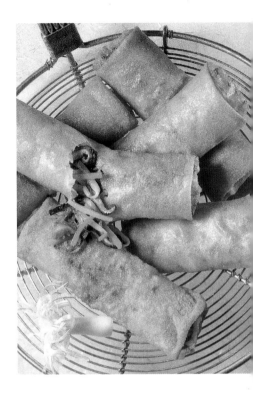

NUTRITIONAL INFORMATION

Calories	186
Protein	4g
Carbohydrate	18g
Sugars	2g
Fat	11g
Saturates	1g

INGREDIENTS

2 scallions, trimmed, plus extra
to garnish
5 dried Chinese mushrooms or
fresh open-cap mushrooms
1 large carrot
2 oz/55 g canned bamboo shoots
2 oz/55 g Napa cabbage
2 tbsp vegetable oil, plus extra for
deep-frying
generous 2 cups bean sprouts
1 tbsp soy sauce
salt
12 spring roll wrappers
1 egg, beaten

cook's tip

If spring roll wrappers are not available in your local store, you can substitute sheets of phyllo pastry for them in Step 3. Handle the pastry gently, because it breaks easily.

1 To make the garnish, make several cuts into the trimmed end of a scallion and place in a bowl of iced water until the tassels open out. Place the mushrooms in a small bowl and cover with warm water. Let soak for 20–25 minutes, then drain and squeeze out the excess water. Remove the coarse centers and slice the mushroom caps thinly.

Cut the carrot and bamboo shoots into very thin julienne strips. Chop the scallions and shred the Napa cabbage.

2 Heat 2 tablespoons of oil in a preheated wok. Add the mushrooms, carrot, and bamboo shoots and stir-fry for 2 minutes. Add the scallions, Napa cabbage, bean sprouts, and soy sauce. Season

to taste with salt and stir-fry for 2 minutes. Cool.

3 Divide the mixture into 12 equal portions and place one portion on the edge of each spring roll wrapper. Fold in the sides and roll each one up, brushing the join with beaten egg to seal. Heat the oil for deep-frying in a large, heavy-bottomed pan to

350–375°F/180–190°C, or until a cube of bread browns in 30 seconds. Add the spring rolls, in batches, and cook for 4–5 minutes, or until golden and crispy. Take care that the oil is not too hot or the rolls will brown on the outside before cooking on the inside. Drain on paper towels. Keep warm. Garnish with scallion tassels and serve.

lattice pie

cook: 1 hr **prep: 30 mins** **serves 4**

variation

Egg glaze gives the dough a shiny finish. If you prefer a matt finish, brush with milk rather than beaten egg.

This pretty pie, with its lattice effect revealing the pale green spinach filling, looks every bit as good as it tastes. Serve warm or cold, accompanied by mixed salad greens.

INGREDIENTS

butter, for greasing

2 quantities Rich Unsweetened Pastry Dough (see page 13), chilled

plain flour, for dusting

lightly beaten egg, to glaze

FILLING

1 lb/450 g frozen spinach, thawed

2 tbsp olive oil

1 large onion, chopped

2 garlic cloves, finely chopped

2 eggs, lightly beaten

8 oz/225 g ricotta cheese

½ cup freshly grated Parmesan cheese

pinch of freshly grated nutmeg

salt and pepper

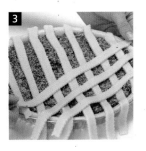

cook's tip

When preparing dough for a tart pan, roll out away from you lightly in one direction only. Rotate the pastry in between strokes to ensure an even thickness.

1 Preheat the oven to 400°F/200°C. To make the filling, drain the spinach and squeeze out as much moisture as possible. Heat the olive oil in a large, heavy-bottomed skillet. Add the onion and cook, stirring occasionally, for 5 minutes, or until softened. Add the garlic and spinach and cook, stirring occasionally, for 10 minutes.

Remove the skillet from the heat, cool slightly, then beat in the eggs and the ricotta and Parmesan cheeses. Season to taste with nutmeg, salt, and pepper.

2 Lightly grease a 9-inch/23-cm loose-bottomed tart pan with butter. Roll out two-thirds of the Pastry Dough on a lightly floured counter

and use it to line the tart pan, leaving it overhanging the sides. Spoon in the spinach mixture, spreading it evenly over the bottom.

3 Roll out the remaining Pastry Dough on a lightly floured counter and cut into ¼-inch/5-mm strips. Arrange the strips in a lattice pattern on top of the pie,

pressing the ends securely to seal. Trim any excess dough. Brush with the egg glaze and bake in the preheated oven for about 45 minutes, or until golden brown. Transfer to a wire rack to cool slightly before removing from the tin.

mushroom & onion quiche

serves 4 **prep: 40 mins, plus 1 hr** ⏲ **chilling/cooling** **cook: 1 hr 15 mins** ⏱

Unusually, this quiche does not contain any cheese. For the best flavor, use a mixture of several different types of mushrooms. Many different varieties of "wild" exotic mushrooms are cultivated nowadays with no discernible loss of flavor.

INGREDIENTS

butter, for greasing

1 quantity Rich Unsweetened Pastry Dough (see page 13), chilled

plain flour, for dusting

FILLING

¼ cup unsalted butter

3 red onions, halved and sliced

12 oz/350 g mixed exotic mushrooms, such as ceps, chanterelles, and morels

2 tsp chopped fresh thyme

1 egg

2 egg yolks

generous ⅓ cup heavy cream

salt and pepper

variation

Try making this quiche with other mushrooms such as shiitake, flat mushrooms or oyster mushrooms.

cook's tip

If you are in a hurry, you can use ready-prepared shortcrust pastry dough, but if it is frozen, make sure that you thaw it thoroughly before use.

1 Preheat the oven to 375°F/190°C, then lightly grease a 9-inch/23-cm loose-bottomed quiche pan with butter. Roll out the Pastry Dough on a lightly floured counter and line the pan. Prick the bottom and chill for 30 minutes. Line with foil and dried beans and bake in the preheated oven for 25 minutes. Remove the foil and beans and cool on a wire rack. Reduce the oven temperature to 350°F/180°C.

2 To make the filling, melt the butter in a large, heavy-bottomed skillet. Add the onions, cover, and cook over very low heat, stirring occasionally, for 20 minutes. Add the mushrooms and chopped thyme and cook, stirring occasionally, for an additional 10 minutes. Spoon the mixture into the cooled tart shell and place the pan on a cookie sheet.

3 Lightly beat the egg with the egg yolks and cream and season to taste with salt and pepper. Pour the mixture over the mushroom filling and bake in the oven for 20 minutes, or until the filling is set and golden. Serve hot or at room temperature.

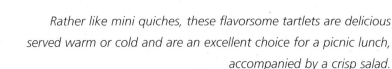

leek & onion tartlets

serves 6　　**prep: 30 mins, plus 1 hr chilling/cooling**　　**cook: 40 mins**

Rather like mini quiches, these flavorsome tartlets are delicious served warm or cold and are an excellent choice for a picnic lunch, accompanied by a crisp salad.

INGREDIENTS

butter, for greasing
1 quantity Rich Unsweetened Pastry
Dough (see page 13)
all-purpose flour, for dusting

FILLING

2 tbsp unsalted butter
1 onion, thinly sliced
1 lb/450 g leeks, thinly sliced
2 tsp chopped fresh thyme
½ cup grated Swiss cheese
3 eggs
1¼ cups heavy cream
salt and pepper

NUTRITIONAL INFORMATION	
Calories	.575
Protein	.11g
Carbohydrate	.28g
Sugars	.5g
Fat	.47g
Saturates	.28g

variation

Substitute 1 lb/450 g of sliced zucchinis for the leeks for a slightly milder version of these tartlets.

1 Preheat the oven to 375°F/190°C. Lightly grease 6 x 4-inch/10-cm small tart pans with butter. Roll out the Pastry Dough on a lightly floured counter and stamp out 6 circles with a 5-inch/13-cm cutter. Ease the dough into the tart pans, prick the bottoms and chill for 30 minutes. Line the tart shells with foil and dried beans, then place on a cookie sheet and bake for 8 minutes. Remove the foil and beans and bake for an additional 2 minutes. Transfer the pans to a wire rack to cool. Reduce the oven temperature to 350°F/180°C.

2 Meanwhile, make the filling. Melt the butter in a large, heavy-bottomed skillet. Add the onion and cook, stirring constantly, for 5 minutes, or until softened. Add the leeks and thyme and cook, stirring, for 10 minutes, or until softened. Divide the leek mixture between the tart shells, then sprinkle with Swiss cheese.

3 Lightly beat the eggs with the cream and season to taste with salt and pepper. Place the tart pans on a cookie sheet and divide the egg mixture between them. Bake in the preheated oven for 15 minutes, or until the filling is set and golden brown. Transfer to a wire rack to cool slightly before removing from the pans and serving.

tomato & onion bake with eggs

cook: 1 hr   **prep: 10 mins**   **serves 4–6**

This nourishing and flavorsome bake is just the right thing for a weekend lunch on a cold winter's day. It is a substantial meal, especially if served with a basket full of crusty bread rolls.

NUTRITIONAL INFORMATION

Calories	307
Protein	11g
Carbohydrate	28g
Sugars	11g
Fat	18g
Saturates	9g

INGREDIENTS

¼ cup butter, plus extra
for greasing

2 large onions, thinly sliced

1 lb 2 oz/500 g tomatoes,
peeled and sliced

4 oz/115 g fresh white bread crumbs

salt and pepper

4 eggs

variation

For added spice, seed and slice 2 red bell peppers and add once the onions have softened. Cook for 10 minutes, then stir in a pinch of cayenne pepper.

1 Preheat the oven to 350°F/180°C, then grease an ovenproof dish with butter.

2 Melt 3 tablespoons of the butter in a heavy-bottomed skillet over low heat. Add the sliced onions and cook, stirring occasionally, for 5 minutes, or until softened.

3 Layer the onions, tomatoes, and bread crumbs in the dish, seasoning each layer with salt and pepper to taste. Dot the remaining butter on top and bake in the preheated oven for 40 minutes.

4 Remove the bake from the oven and make 4 hollows in the mixture with the back of a spoon. Crack 1 egg into each hollow. Return the dish to the oven for an additional 15 minutes, or until the eggs are just set. Serve immediately.

pizza alla siciliana

⏱ **cook: 40 mins**   ⏱ **prep: 25 mins**   **serves 2**

NUTRITIONAL INFORMATION

Calories	1210
Protein	52g
Carbohydrate	144g
Sugars	11g
Fat	51g
Saturates	18g

variation

If you like a nutty taste to your pizzas, substitute a scant ¼ cup of pine nuts for the capers in Step 3.

Olives, roasted eggplants, cheese, and a rich tomato sauce are gloriously combined in this classic vegetarian pizza—a sure favorite for parties and picnics.

INGREDIENTS

olive oil, for brushing

2 x 10-inch/25-cm Pizza Doughs (see page 13)

TOMATO SAUCE

7 oz/200 g canned chopped tomatoes

5 tbsp strained tomatoes

1 garlic glove, finely chopped

1 bay leaf

½ tsp dried oregano

½ tsp sugar

1 tsp balsamic vinegar

salt and pepper

TOPPING

1 eggplant, thinly sliced

2 tbsp olive oil

6 oz/175 g mozzarella cheese, sliced

2 oz/55 g marinated, pitted black olives

1 tbsp drained capers

4 tbsp freshly grated Parmesan cheese

cook's tip

For a really delicious topping, look for *mozzarella di bufala*—cheese made with water buffalo's milk—which has the finest flavor and texture.

1 Preheat the oven to 400°F/200°C. To make the tomato sauce, place all the ingredients in a heavy-bottomed pan, season to taste, and bring to a boil. Reduce the heat and simmer, stirring occasionally, for about 20 minutes, or until thickened and reduced. Remove from the heat, discard the bay leaf, and let cool.

2 Meanwhile, brush a cookie sheet with the oil. Brush the eggplant slices with the oil, then spread them out on the cookie sheet. Bake in the preheated oven for 5 minutes, then turn the slices over and bake for an additional 5–10 minutes. Transfer the slices to paper towels to drain. Increase the oven temperature to 425°F/220°C.

3 Brush 2 cookie sheets or pizza pans with oil and place the Pizza Doughs on them. Divide the tomato sauce between them, spreading it almost to the edges. Arrange the eggplant on top and cover with mozzarella. Top with olives and capers and sprinkle with Parmesan. Bake for 15–20 minutes, or until golden. Serve immediately.

roasted vegetable pizza

serves 2   **prep: 30 mins, plus 30 mins cooling**   **cook: 35 mins**

This flamboyant pizza looks like a real work of art and will turn any occasion into a party. Its high fresh vegetable content makes it an especially nutritious and satisfying dish.

INGREDIENTS

4 garlic cloves

2 red onions, cut into wedges

1 orange bell pepper, seeded and cut into 8 strips

1 yellow bell pepper, seeded and cut into 8 strips

4 baby zucchini, halved lengthwise

4 baby eggplants, cut lengthwise into 4 slices

salt and pepper

½ cup olive oil, plus extra for brushing

1 tbsp balsamic vinegar

2 tbsp fresh basil leaves, plus extra to garnish

2 x 10-inch/25-cm Pizza Doughs (see page 13)

1 quantity Tomato Sauce (see page 83)

6 oz/175 g goat cheese, diced

NUTRITIONAL INFORMATION	
Calories	1490
Protein	42g
Carbohydrate	173g
Sugars	30g
Fat	76g
Saturates	17g

variation

Any firm vegetables can be used for the topping. If you can't find any goat cheese, substitute feta cheese.

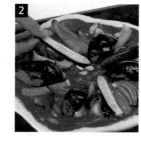

cook's tip

When using fresh leaves such as basil or arugula on pizzas, add them after cooking, otherwise they will lose their moisture and wilt or burn.

1 Preheat the oven to 400°F/200°C. Spread the garlic, onions, bell peppers, zucchini, and eggplants in a roasting pan. Season to taste with salt and pepper. Mix the oil, vinegar, and basil together in a pitcher and pour the mixture over the vegetables, tossing well to coat. Roast in the preheated oven for 15 minutes, turning once or twice during cooking. Let cool. Increase the oven temperature to 425°F/220°C.

2 Brush 2 cookie sheets or pizza pans with oil, place the Pizza Doughs on them and divide the Tomato Sauce between them, spreading it almost to the edges. Peel off the skins from the bell pepper strips. Peel and slice the garlic. Arrange the vegetables on top of the Tomato Sauce, then sprinkle with the goat cheese. Drizzle over the roasting juices.

3 Bake in the oven for 15–20 minutes, or until golden. Garnish with fresh basil and serve immediately.

penne with zucchini & walnuts

cook: 35 mins   **prep: 15 mins**   **serves 4**

NUTRITIONAL INFORMATION	
Calories	.635
Protein	.19g
Carbohydrate	.82g
Sugars	.8g
Fat	.29g
Saturates	.8g

variation

Other types of pasta would also work well in this dish. Try using farfalle, spaghetti, tagliatelle, or pappardelle.

Pasta is wonderfully versatile and goes with a wide range of vegetables. Here, it is served with a creamy, mouthwatering sauce made from onion, zucchini, walnuts, and herbs.

INGREDIENTS

2 tbsp butter	13 oz/375 g dried penne
3 tbsp olive oil	generous ½ cup chopped walnuts
2 red onions, thinly sliced	3 tbsp chopped fresh flatleaf parsley
1 lb/450 g zucchini, thinly sliced	2 tbsp sour cream
salt and pepper	2 tbsp freshly grated Parmesan cheese

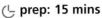

cook's tip

For perfect pasta, start checking for tenderness when it has been cooking for about 7 minutes by breaking off a small piece and biting it. As soon as it is ready, turn off the heat and drain.

1 Melt the butter with the olive oil in a large, heavy-bottomed skillet. Add the sliced onions, cover, and cook over low heat, stirring occasionally, for 5 minutes, or until softened. Add the sliced zucchini and stir to mix well. Cover and cook, stirring occasionally, for 15–20 minutes, or until the vegetables are very tender.

2 Bring a pan of lightly salted water to a boil. Add the pasta, return to a boil and simmer for 8–10 minutes, or until tender, but still firm to the bite (al dente).

3 Meanwhile, stir the walnuts, parsley, and sour cream into the zucchini mixture and season to taste with salt and pepper. When the pasta is al dente, drain and tip into a large serving dish. Add the zucchini mixture and toss well. Sprinkle the Parmesan cheese over the pasta and serve immediately.

hot chile pasta

Chiles are not often associated with Italian cooking, but some regions of the country grow fiery hot chiles nicknamed "little devils." This dish is suitable for vegans, if served without cheese.

INGREDIENTS

2 garlic cloves, finely chopped

2 fresh red chiles

1 lb 4 oz/550 g strained tomatoes or
crushed plum tomatoes

7 oz/200 g canned chopped
plum tomatoes

generous ¾ cup dry white wine

4 tsp sun-dried tomato paste

salt and pepper

1 lb/450 g dried gemelli

3 tbsp chopped fresh flatleaf parsley

freshly grated Parmesan cheese,
to garnish (optional)

NUTRITIONAL INFORMATION

Calories	.320
Protein	.10g
Carbohydrate	.61g
Sugars	.7g
Fat	.4g
Saturates	.0g

cook's tip

Gemelli, meaning "twins," are made from two short pieces of pasta twisted together. You can use any small pasta shapes for this dish.

1 Put the garlic into a pan with the whole chiles, strained tomatoes, chopped tomatoes, wine, and tomato paste and bring to a boil, stirring occasionally. Reduce the heat, cover, and simmer while you cook the pasta.

2 Bring a large pan of lightly salted water to a boil. Add the pasta, return to a boil, and simmer for 8–10 minutes, or until tender, but still firm to the bite (al dente). Drain and place in a large, warmed serving dish.

3 Remove the chiles from the sauce. If you like a hot spicy flavor, chop one or both and return to the sauce. If you prefer a milder flavor, discard them. Add half the parsley. Season to taste with salt and pepper, then pour the sauce on to the pasta. Toss well, sprinkle with the remaining parsley, and serve immediately, with the Parmesan cheese.

paglia e fieno

cook: 12 mins　　　　**prep: 15 mins**　　　　serves 4

This simple pasta dish, which literally means "straw and hay," makes a quick and easy light summer lunch that is surprisingly tasty. The freshness of the peas perfectly complements the creamy sauce.

NUTRITIONAL INFORMATION	
Calories	.823
Protein	.23g
Carbohydrate	.94g
Sugars	.7g
Fat	.43g
Saturates	.26g

INGREDIENTS

salt and pepper

1 lb/450 g mixed plain and green dried tagliarini or spaghetti

¼ cup unsalted butter

2 lb/900 g fresh peas, shelled

generous ¾ cup heavy cream

½ cup freshly grated romano cheese, plus extra to serve

pinch of freshly grated nutmeg

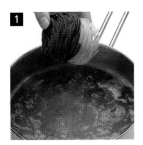

cook's tip

Although peas freeze exceptionally well, they have neither the flavor nor the texture of fresh peas, so it is best to make this dish when peas are in season.

1 Bring a pan of lightly salted water to a boil. Add the pasta, return to a boil, and simmer for 8–10 minutes, or until tender, but still firm to the bite (al dente).

2 Meanwhile, melt the butter in a large, heavy-bottomed pan. Add the peas and cook over low heat, stirring frequently, for 4–5 minutes. Pour in ⅔ cup of the cream and stir to mix well. Bring to a boil and simmer for 1 minute.

3 When the pasta is al dente, drain well and add to the peas. Pour in the remaining cream, then add the romano cheese and season to taste with nutmeg, salt, and pepper. Toss well, then transfer to a warmed serving dish and serve immediately with extra romano cheese.

golden macaroni cheese

serves 4   **prep: 15 mins** ⟳   **cook: 20 mins** ⟳

Always a useful pantry stand-by, macaroni in a cheese sauce can still be a little stodgy and dull. Adding some extra ingredients—onions, tomatoes, and eggs—livens this traditional dish up, and makes it a little more colorful and interesting.

INGREDIENTS

salt	**CHEESE SAUCE**
7 oz/200 g dried elbow macaroni	**3 tbsp butter**
1 onion, sliced	**5 tbsp all-purpose flour**
4 hard-cooked eggs, cut into fourths	**2½ cups milk**
4 cherry tomatoes, halved	**scant 1½ cups grated Red**
3 tbsp dried bread crumbs	**Leicester cheese**
2 tbsp finely grated Red	**pinch of cayenne pepper**
Leicester cheese	

NUTRITIONAL INFORMATION

Calories	.618
Protein	.29g
Carbohydrate	.58g
Sugars	.11g
Fat	.32g
Saturates	.18g

variation

For a little extra texture, add 7 oz/ 200 g drained canned corn kernels with the hard-cooked eggs in Step 3.

cook's tip

Always remove the pan from the heat before stirring in the grated cheese, otherwise the sauce will have a thick, rubbery consistency.

1 Bring a large pan of lightly salted water to a boil. Add the macaroni and sliced onion, return to a boil and cook for 8–10 minutes, or until the pasta is tender, but still firm to the bite (al dente). Drain well and tip the macaroni and onion into an ovenproof dish.

2 To make the cheese sauce, melt the butter in a pan. Stir in the flour and cook, stirring constantly, for 1–2 minutes. Remove the pan from the heat and gradually whisk in the milk. Return the pan to the heat and bring to a boil, whisking constantly. Simmer for 2 minutes, or until the sauce is thick and glossy. Remove the pan from the heat, stir in the cheese, and season to taste with cayenne and salt.

3 Pour the sauce over the macaroni, add the eggs, and mix lightly. Arrange the tomato halves on top. Mix the bread crumbs with the finely grated cheese and sprinkle over the surface. Cook under a preheated hot broiler for 3–4 minutes, or until the topping is golden and bubbling. Serve immediately.

spanish omelet

⏲ cook: 20 mins   ⏱ prep: 20 mins   serves 4

This is an incredibly adaptable dish and you can incorporate leftover and fresh vegetables of your choice. It is easy to put together, and makes a filling and nutritious supper dish.

INGREDIENTS

2 tbsp olive oil

1 Spanish onion, chopped

2 garlic cloves, finely chopped

1 red bell pepper, seeded and diced

9 oz/250 g zucchini, thinly sliced

2 tomatoes, peeled and diced

12 oz/350 g boiled potatoes,

diced (optional)

6 eggs

4 tbsp milk

2 tsp chopped fresh tarragon

salt and pepper

generous ¾ cup grated Cheddar cheese

variation

If you are not cooking for vegetarians, you can add 4 oz/115 g of cooked, peeled prawns or 7 oz/200 g of tuna with the potatoes in Step 1.

cook's tip

If you do not have a skillet with a heatproof handle, cover the handle with a double layer of foil, but be very careful that it doesn't slip out as you lift the skillet up.

1 Heat the oil in a large, heavy-bottomed skillet with a flameproof handle. Add the onion and cook, stirring occasionally, for 5 minutes, or until softened. Add the garlic, red bell pepper, and zucchini and cook, stirring frequently, for an additional 5 minutes. Add the tomatoes and potatoes and cook, stirring frequently, for 3 minutes.

2 Beat the eggs with the milk and tarragon in a bowl and season to taste with salt and pepper. Pour the egg mixture into the skillet and cook, without stirring, until the eggs begin to set and the underside is golden brown.

3 Sprinkle the cheese evenly over the surface and place the skillet under a preheated hot broiler. Cook the omelet for 3–4 minutes, or until the cheese has melted and the top is golden brown. Cut into wedges to serve.

potato omelets

serves 4   **prep: 20 mins** ⟲   **cook: 25 mins** ⟲

These quick, chunky omelets have pieces of potato cooked into the egg mixture and are then filled with feta cheese, spinach, and plain yogurt, flavored with just a hint of fennel. They make an easy and warming meal, packed with valuable nutrients such as folic acid, vitamin C, and calcium.

INGREDIENTS

5 tbsp butter

6 waxy potatoes, diced

3 garlic cloves, crushed

1 tsp paprika

2 tomatoes, peeled, seeded and diced

12 eggs

pepper

FILLING

8 oz/225 g fresh baby spinach

1 tsp fennel seeds

4½ oz/125 g feta cheese, diced

4 tbsp plain yogurt

NUTRITIONAL INFORMATION

Calories	564
Protein	. . . . .30g
Carbohydrate	. . . . .25g
Sugars	. . . . .6g
Fat	. . . . .39g
Saturates	. . . . .19g

variation

Use any other cheese, such as blue cheese, instead of the feta, and blanched broccoli in place of the baby spinach, if you prefer.

cook's tip

Whisk the eggs well to make sure that the omelets are fluffy and light. They should be served as soon as possible after leaving the omelet pan.

1 Melt 2 tablespoons of the butter in a large, heavy-bottomed skillet over low heat, add the diced potatoes and cook, stirring constantly, for 7–10 minutes, or until golden brown. Transfer to a bowl. Add the garlic, paprika, and tomatoes to the skillet, cook for 2 minutes, then add to the potatoes.

2 Whisk the eggs together and season to taste with pepper. Pour the eggs into the potatoes and mix well.

3 To make the filling, cook the spinach in boiling water for 1 minute, or until just wilted. Drain and refresh under cold running water. Pat dry with paper towels and transfer to a bowl. Stir in the fennel seeds, feta cheese, and yogurt.

4 Heat one fourth of the remaining butter in a 6-inch/15-cm omelet pan. Ladle one fourth of the egg and potato mixture into the omelet pan. Cook, turning once, for 2 minutes, or until set. Transfer the omelet to a serving plate. Spoon one fourth of the spinach mixture on to one half of the omelet, then fold the omelet in half over the filling and keep warm. Repeat to make 4 omelets. Transfer to warmed serving plates and serve immediately.

main meals

The mouthwatering collection of vegetable main meals in this chapter would convert even the most tenacious carnivore. Recipes range from rich stews and casseroles to light-as-air soufflés, and from fabulous burgers and sausages to traditional risottos. There are economical but filling, midweek family supper dishes, such as Vegetable Curry (see page 107), Cheese & Tomato Bake (see page 112 and Vegetable Crumble (see page 117), as well as more sophisticated recipes for when you have more time or are entertaining. Try Phyllo Pockets (see page 127) or Artichoke Heart Soufflé (see page 122), for example.

Protein-packed pulses play an important part in the vegetarian diet and this chapter includes some starring roles for peas, beans, and lentils in stews, casseroles, bakes, pies, burgers, and risottos. Many other vegetables feature, too—from Stuffed Bell Peppers with Cheese (see page 105) to Mushroom Gougère (see page 128) and from Spinach & Cheese Crêpes (see page 132) to Caribbean Rice & Peas (see page 149).

There are dishes to suit everyone and recipes were inspired by the best of vegetarian cooking from all over the world. The variety is huge—French, Kenyan, and Italian stews, Chinese Braised Vegetables (see page 113), Indian curry, Spanish paella, Italian pasta, North African couscous, Greek moussaka, and Glamorgan sausages. Whether your taste is for the hot and spicy, crisp and refreshing, rich and heart-warming, or subtle and aromatic, you are sure to find precisely the main meal that you require.

cold weather casserole

cook: 1 hr 15 mins   **prep: 20 mins**   **serves 6**

NUTRITIONAL INFORMATION

Calories 345

Protein 9g

Carbohydrate 43g

Sugars 6g

Fat 17g

Saturates 10g

variation

If you like, replace the rutabaga with 2 parsnips, sliced, and the butter beans with canned kidney beans.

Heart-warming comfort food on a chilly evening, this is a rich casserole of root vegetables, served with tasty parsley dumplings. This dish is suitable for both vegetarians and vegans.

INGREDIENTS

¼ cup butter or vegetarian margarine

2 leeks, sliced

2 carrots, sliced

2 potatoes, cut into bite-size pieces

1 rutabaga, cut into bite-size pieces

2 zucchini, sliced

1 fennel bulb, halved and sliced

2 tbsp all-purpose flour

15 oz/425 g canned lima beans

2½ cups Vegetable Stock
(see page 13)

2 tbsp tomato paste

1 tsp dried thyme

2 bay leaves

salt and pepper

DUMPLINGS

generous ¾ cup self-rising flour

pinch of salt

½ cup vegetarian suet

2 tbsp chopped fresh parsley

about 4 tbsp water

cook's tip

Vegetarian suet, made from hard vegetable fat, can be used in the same way as beef suet. Some margarines contain animal fats, so vegetarians should look for labels marked "vegetarian margarine."

1 Melt the butter in a large, heavy-bottomed pan over low heat. Add the leeks, carrots, potatoes, rutabaga, zucchini, and fennel and cook, stirring occasionally, for 10 minutes. Stir in the flour and cook, stirring constantly, for 1 minute. Stir in the can juice from the beans, the Stock, tomato paste, thyme, and bay leaves and season to taste with salt and pepper. Bring to a boil, stirring constantly, then cover and simmer for 10 minutes.

2 Meanwhile, make the dumplings. Sift the flour and salt into a bowl. Stir in the suet and parsley, then add enough water to bind to a soft dough. Divide the dough into 8 pieces and roll into balls.

3 Add the lima beans and dumplings to the pan, cover, and simmer for an additional 30 minutes. Remove and discard the bay leaf before serving.

kenyan dengu

This mildly spiced mung bean stew is economical, filling, and easy to make—a perfect dish for a midweek family supper. This dish is suitable for both vegetarians and vegans.

INGREDIENTS

1¼ cups mung beans, soaked overnight
in enough water to cover

2 tbsp corn oil

1 onion, chopped

2 garlic cloves, finely chopped

2 tbsp tomato paste

1 red bell pepper, seeded and diced

1 green bell pepper, seeded and diced

1 fresh red chile, seeded and
finely chopped

1¼ cups Vegetable Stock
(see page 13) or water

NUTRITIONAL INFORMATION

Calories	254
Protein	17g
Carbohydrate	34g
Sugars	8g
Fat	6g
Saturates	1g

1   Drain the mung beans, place in a pan and cover with water. Bring to a boil, cover, and simmer for 1–1¼ hours, or until the beans are tender. Drain well, return to the pan, and mash thoroughly until smooth.

2   Heat the oil in another pan. Add the onion and cook, stirring occasionally, for 10 minutes, or until golden. Add the garlic, cook for 2 minutes, then add the tomato paste and cook, stirring, for 3 minutes.

3   Stir the mashed beans into the onion mixture. Add the bell peppers, chile, and Stock, stir well, and simmer gently for 10 minutes. Transfer to a warmed serving dish and serve immediately.

variation

If you want to add a little extra flavor to this dish, stir in 8 oz/225 g of shredded spinach leaves 3–4 minutes before the end of cooking in Step 3.

vegetable & lentil casserole

cook: 2 hours   **prep: 15 minutes**   **serves 4**

This easy, one-pot dish cooks slowly so that the flavors mingle deliciously. The Puy lentils keep their shape and texture better than other varieties. This dish is suitable for both vegetarians and vegans.

NUTRITIONAL INFORMATION	
Calories	273
Protein	18g
Carbohydrate	50g
Sugars	9g
Fat	2g
Saturates	0g

INGREDIENTS

1 onion

10 cloves

generous 1 cup Puy or green lentils

1 bay leaf

6¼ cups Vegetable Stock
(see page 13)

2 leeks, sliced

2 potatoes, diced

2 carrots, chopped

3 zucchini, sliced

1 celery stalk, chopped

1 red bell pepper, seeded and chopped

salt and pepper

1 tbsp lemon juice

cook's tip

Unlike other pulses, lentils do not require soaking before they are cooked, making them a convenient stock food for pulse-based meals.

1 Preheat the oven to 350°F/180°C. Press the cloves into the onion. Put the lentils into a large casserole, add the onion and bay leaf, and pour in the Stock. Cover and bake in the preheated oven for 1 hour.

2 Remove the casserole from the oven. Take out the onion and discard the cloves. Slice the onion and return it to the casserole with the leeks, potatoes, carrots, zucchini, celery, and red bell pepper. Stir thoroughly and season to taste with salt and pepper. Cover and return to the oven for 1 hour.

3 Remove and discard the bay leaf. Stir in the lemon juice and serve straight from the casserole.

provençal bean stew

serves 4 | **prep: 20 mins** | **cook: 2 hrs 30 mins**

Bursting with Mediterranean flavors, this colorful stew is delicious served with garlic bread. It is suitable for vegetarians and vegans.

INGREDIENTS

2 cups dried pinto beans, soaked
overnight in enough water to cover

2 tbsp olive oil

2 onions, sliced

2 garlic cloves, finely chopped

1 red bell pepper, seeded and sliced

1 yellow bell pepper, seeded and sliced

14 oz/400 g canned chopped tomatoes

2 tbsp tomato paste

1 tbsp torn fresh basil leaves

2 tsp chopped fresh thyme

2 tsp chopped fresh rosemary

1 bay leaf

salt and pepper

2 oz/55 g black olives,

pitted and halved

2 tbsp chopped fresh parsley,

to garnish

NUTRITIONAL INFORMATION

Calories 420

Protein 22g

Carbohydrate 64g

Sugars 12g

Fat 9g

Saturates 1g

---

variation

You could substitute other beans,
such as borlotti, cannellini, or Great
Northern beans, or use a mixture
of different types.

cook's tip

When using beans, always
follow package instructions for
soaking and cooking. If you
use borlotti beans, boil them
vigorously for 15 minutes
before simmering in Step 1.

1 Drain the beans. Place in a large pan, add enough cold water to cover, and bring to a boil. Reduce the heat, then cover and simmer for 1¼–1½ hours, or until almost tender. Drain, reserving 1¼ cups of the cooking liquid.

2 Heat the oil in a heavy-bottomed pan. Add the onions and cook, stirring occasionally, for 5 minutes, or until softened. Add the garlic and bell peppers. Cook, stirring frequently, for 10 minutes.

3 Add the tomatoes and their juices, the reserved cooking liquid, tomato paste, basil, thyme, rosemary, bay leaf, and beans and season to taste with salt and pepper. Cover and simmer for 40 minutes. Add the olives and simmer for 5 minutes. Transfer to a warmed serving dish, sprinkle with the parsley, and serve immediately.

serves 6   **prep: 30 mins**   **cook: 55 mins**

Use onions that are all about the same size for even cooking. Serve this dish with rice and one of the salads on pages 196–210. If silken bean curd is substituted for the yogurt, it is suitable for vegans.

INGREDIENTS

¼ cup raisins

6 onions

1 tbsp corn oil

1 garlic clove, finely chopped

1 lb/450 g fresh spinach, coarse
stems removed

salt

½ cup plain yogurt

scant ¼ cup pine nuts, toasted

pinch of freshly grated nutmeg

2 tbsp fresh whole-wheat bread crumbs

NUTRITIONAL INFORMATION

Calories 188

Protein 7g

Carbohydrate 28g

Sugars 21g

Fat 6g

Saturates 1g

cook's tip

When stuffing vegetables, to avoid burning your fingers, let the hot stuffing mixture cool slightly before placing it inside the vegetables.

1 Preheat the oven to 350°F/180°C. Place the raisins in a bowl, cover with water, and reserve. Cut a thin slice off the bottoms of the onions so that they stand level. Cut off a ½-inch/1-cm slice from the tops. Scoop out the flesh with a teaspoon, leaving a ½-inch/1-cm thick shell. Set a steamer over a pan of boiling water, arrange the onion shells inside, cover, and steam for 10–15 minutes, or until tender. Remove from the heat and reserve.

2 Chop the scooped-out flesh. Heat the corn oil in a skillet, add the chopped onion, and cook, stirring occasionally, for 5 minutes, or until softened. Stir in the garlic and cook for 2 minutes. Add the spinach, cover, and cook for 3 minutes, or until wilted. Season with salt and cook, uncovered, stirring occasionally, for 5 minutes, or until the liquid evaporates. Remove from the heat.

3 Drain the raisins. Add them to the spinach mixture with the yogurt, pine nuts, and nutmeg. Drain 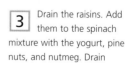 the onion shells and spoon the spinach stuffing into them. Spread the remaining stuffing over the bottom of an ovenproof dish and stand the onions on top. Sprinkle with bread crumbs and bake in the preheated oven for 25 minutes. Place under a preheated hot broiler for 3–4 minutes, or until the bread crumbs are crisp. Serve immediately.

stuffed bell peppers with cheese

cook: 45 mins   **prep: 25 mins**   **serves 4**

A flavorsome mixture of vegetables and rice makes these bell peppers into a meal. Use a mixture of peppers for a colorful display at the supper table, and serve with mixed salad greens.

NUTRITIONAL INFORMATION

Calories	.480
Protein	.14g
Carbohydrate	.59g
Sugars	.14g
Fat	.23g
Saturates	.6g

INGREDIENTS

4 large green, yellow, or red bell peppers

scant 2 cups Vegetable Stock (see page 13)

1 cup long-grain rice

2 tbsp olive oil

1 onion, chopped

2 garlic cloves, finely chopped

4 oz/115 g cremini mushrooms, chopped

4 tomatoes, peeled and chopped

1 carrot, diced

salt and pepper

1 tbsp chopped fresh parsley

3½ oz/100 g goat cheese, crumbled

scant ½ cup pine nuts

¼ cup freshly grated Parmesan cheese

cook's tip

The color of bell peppers depends on what stage of development they are at when they are picked. If you prefer a sweeter taste, pick orange and red bell peppers, which are riper than green bell peppers.

1 Preheat the oven to 375°F/190°C. Cut the bell peppers in half lengthwise and seed. Blanch in a large pan of boiling water for 5 minutes. Remove with a perforated spoon and drain upside down.

2 Pour the Stock into a separate pan, add the rice, and bring to a boil.

Reduce the heat, cover, and simmer for 15 minutes. Remove from the heat and reserve, covered, for 5 minutes, then drain. Heat the oil in a skillet, add the onion, and cook, stirring occasionally, for 5 minutes, or until softened. Add the garlic, mushrooms, tomatoes, and carrot and season to taste. Cover and cook for 5 minutes.

3 Stir the rice, parsley, goat cheese, and pine nuts into the vegetable mixture. Place the bell pepper halves, cut side up, in a roasting pan or ovenproof dish. Divide the rice and vegetable mixture between them. Sprinkle with Parmesan cheese. Bake in the preheated oven for 20 minutes, or until the cheese is golden. Serve.

vegetable curry

cook: 35 mins   **prep: 20 mins**   **serves 4**

The secret of a good curry lies in finding the right balance of spices, both in terms of heat and flavor. Here, the curry paste is enhanced with a selection of individual spices, from warming cumin and mustard seeds to mouthwatering fresh gingerroot and chile. This dish is suitable for both vegetarians and vegans.

variation

For a hotter curry, leave the seeds in the chilli, add an extra fresh chilli, add a pinch of chilli powder with the turmeric in Step 3 or do all of these.

INGREDIENTS

2 tbsp corn oil	2 carrots, sliced
½ tsp cumin seeds	1 cauliflower, cut into florets
½ tsp black mustard seeds	4 oz/115 g green beans, cut in half
1 onion, thinly sliced	2 tomatoes, diced
2 curry leaves	¼ tsp ground turmeric
1 tbsp finely chopped fresh gingerroot	2 oz/55 g peas, thawed if frozen
1 fresh green chile, seeded and finely chopped	salt
2 tbsp curry paste	⅔ cup Vegetable Stock (see page 13)

cook's tip

Frying spice seeds mellows their flavor. When choosing mustard seeds, remember that the darker the seeds, the stronger the flavor—yellow seeds are milder than brown or black seeds.

1 Heat the corn oil in a large, heavy-bottomed pan. Add the cumin seeds and black mustard seeds and cook, stirring constantly, for 1–2 minutes, or until the seeds begin to give off their aroma and pop. Add the sliced onion and curry leaves and cook, stirring frequently, for 5 minutes, or until the onion is softened.

2 Add the gingerroot and chile and cook, stirring frequently, for 1 minute, then stir in the curry paste and cook, stirring, for 4 minutes. Stir in the carrots, cauliflower, and beans and cook, stirring occasionally, for 5 minutes.

3 Add the tomatoes, turmeric, and peas and season to taste with salt. Cook for 2 minutes, then add the peas and cook for an additional 2 minutes. Finally, add the Stock, stir well, cover and simmer for 12 minutes, or until all the vegetables are tender. Serve immediately.

winter couscous

serves 4   prep: 30 mins   cook: 35 mins

This warming, aromatic sweet-and-sour dish is a complete and satisfying main course. Cook the couscous in a steamer over the vegetable stew to add to the flavor, as well as save fuel. This dish is suitable for both vegetarians and vegans.

NUTRITIONAL INFORMATION

Calories 539

Protein 16g

Carbohydrate 101g

Sugars 27g

Fat 11g

Saturates 1g

INGREDIENTS

3 tbsp olive oil	½ tsp ground cinnamon
1 onion, cut into wedges	¼ tsp saffron threads
2 potatoes, cut into chunks	1 tbsp tomato paste
2 carrots, cut into chunks	generous 1¾ cups Vegetable Stock
2 parsnips, cut into chunks	(see page 13)
2 turnips, cut into chunks	10½ oz/300 g canned ful medames,
1 yam (dark sweet potato),	drained and rinsed
cut into chunks	⅓ cup raisins
2 garlic cloves, finely chopped	3 tbsp chopped fresh cilantro
1 tsp ground coriander	salt and pepper
1 tsp ground cumin	12 oz/350 g couscous
½ tsp ground turmeric	chili sauce, to serve
½ tsp ground ginger	

variation

If you wish, substitute other favorite vegetables for the carrots, parsnips, turnips, and yam—though root vegetables give the best flavor.

cook's tip

Lining the steamer with a piece of clean muslin will prevent the fine grains of the couscous from falling through the holes during cooking.

1 Heat the oil in a large pan. Add the onion and cook, stirring occasionally, for 5 minutes, or until softened. Add the potatoes, carrots, parsnips, turnips, and yam and cook, stirring, for 5 minutes.

2 Add the garlic, ground coriander, cumin, turmeric, ginger, cinnamon, and saffron and cook, stirring constantly, for 1 minute. Add the tomato paste and pour in the Stock. Stir in the ful medames, raisins, and fresh cilantro, season to taste with salt and pepper, and bring to a boil. Reduce the heat.

3 Place the couscous in a strainer and rinse under cold running water. Line a steamer with muslin and place it over the pan of vegetables. Tip in the couscous, cover, and simmer for 20 minutes. Transfer the couscous into a warmed serving dish, top with the vegetable stew, and serve with the chili sauce.

vegetable chili

cook: 1 hr 15 mins   **prep: 10 mins**   **serves 4**

variation

Substitute the red bell peppers with yellow bell peppers and peel the eggplant before slicing, if you like.

This dish is hearty and flavorsome and is delicious served on its own. Alternatively, it can be spooned over freshly cooked rice or baked potatoes to make it into a more substantial meal.

INGREDIENTS

1 eggplant, cut into 1-inch/2.5-cm slices

1 tbsp olive oil, plus extra for brushing

1 large red onion, finely chopped

2 red or yellow bell peppers, seeded and finely chopped

3–4 garlic cloves, finely chopped or crushed

1 lb 12 oz/800 g canned chopped tomatoes

1 tbsp mild chili powder

½ tsp ground cumin

½ tsp dried oregano

salt and pepper

2 small zucchini, cut into fourths, lengthwise, and sliced

14 oz/400 g canned kidney beans, drained and rinsed

2 cups water

1 tbsp tomato paste

6 scallions, finely chopped

generous 1 cup grated Cheddar cheese

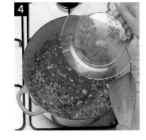

cook's tip

If you prefer your chili dish with a little extra heat, you can stir in a little more chili powder when you adjust the seasoning in Step 5.

1 Brush the eggplant slices on one side with olive oil. Heat half the oil in a large, heavy-bottomed skillet over medium–high heat. Add the eggplant slices, oiled-side up, and cook for 5–6 minutes, or until browned on one side. Turn the slices over, cook on the other side until browned, and transfer to a plate. Cut into bite-size pieces.

2 Heat the remaining oil in a large pan over medium heat. Add the onion and bell peppers and cook, stirring occasionally, for 3–4 minutes, or until the onion is softened, but not browned.

3 Add the garlic and cook for an additional 2–3 minutes, or until the onion is beginning to color.

4 Add the tomatoes, chili powder, cumin, and oregano. Season to taste with salt and pepper. Bring just to a boil, reduce the heat, cover, and simmer gently for 15 minutes.

5 Add the zucchini, eggplant pieces, and kidney beans. Stir in the water and the tomato paste. Return to a boil, then cover and continue simmering for 45 minutes, or until the vegetables are tender. Taste and adjust the seasoning if necessary. Ladle into warmed serving bowls and top with scallions and cheese.

cheese & tomato bake

serves 4   **prep: 15 mins**   **cook: 40 mins**

A juicy combination of vegetables concealed beneath a crisp topping needs only mixed salad greens and a few crusty bread rolls to make a substantial family supper dish.

INGREDIENTS

2 tbsp olive oil

2 onions, sliced

1 garlic clove, finely chopped

12 oz/350 g zucchini, sliced

1 tsp chopped fresh thyme

1 tbsp torn fresh basil leaves

salt and pepper

4 beefsteak tomatoes, peeled and sliced

½ quantity Cheese Sauce (see page 90), made with Cheddar cheese

½ cup grated Cheddar cheese

NUTRITIONAL INFORMATION

Calories 324

Protein 14g

Carbohydrate 19g

Sugars 10g

Fat 22g

Saturates 11g

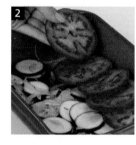

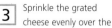

1 Preheat the oven to 350°C/180°C. Heat the olive oil in a heavy-bottomed skillet. Add the onions and cook, stirring occasionally, for 5 minutes, or until softened. Add the garlic, sliced zucchini, thyme, and basil leaves and season to taste with salt and pepper. Cook, stirring occasionally, for 5 minutes.

2 Spoon half the onion and zucchini mixture into a large ovenproof dish. Arrange the tomato slices on top and cover with the remaining onion and zucchini mixture, then pour in the Cheese Sauce.

3 Sprinkle the grated cheese evenly over the vegetables. Bake in the preheated oven for 30 minutes, until golden brown and crisp, then serve.

cook's tip

Beefsteak tomatoes are better for layered bakes than smaller tomatoes because they hold their shape and texture when baked. Choose firm tomatoes with a fresh fragrance.

chinese braised vegetables

cook: 10 mins   **prep: 10 mins**   **serves 4**

Quickly prepared and packed with flavor, this dish is first stir-fried and the vegetables are then briefly braised to finish them off. It is suitable for both vegetarians and vegans.

NUTRITIONAL INFORMATION

Calories	190
Protein	12g
Carbohydrate	7g
Sugars	2g
Fat	13g
Saturates	4g

INGREDIENTS

¼ oz/10 g Chinese dried mushrooms

3 tbsp peanut or corn oil

8 oz/225 g firm bean curd (drained weight), cut into cubes

6 oz/175 g Napa cabbage, shredded

3 oz/85 g canned sliced bamboo shoots, drained and rinsed

3 oz/85 g straw mushrooms, halved

3 oz/85 g snow peas

½ tsp brown sugar

1 tbsp dark soy sauce

dash of sesame oil

cook's tip

Bean curd, also known as tofu, comes in a variety of forms. Firm, marinated and smoked bean curd are all suitable for stir-frying.

1 Put the Chinese dried mushrooms into a small bowl, cover with cold water, and let soak for 20 minutes. Drain, then cut off and discard any hard stems.

2 Heat the oil in a preheated wok. Add the bean curd cubes and stir-fry for 2–4 minutes, or until browned. Remove from the wok with a perforated spoon and reserve.

3 Add the Chinese dried mushrooms, Napa cabbage, bamboo shoots, straw mushrooms, and snow peas to the wok and stir-fry for 2 minutes. Return the bean curd to the wok and add the sugar and soy sauce. Stir for 1 minute, then cover and braise for 3 minutes. Sprinkle with a dash of sesame oil before serving.

italian vegetable stew

serves 4   **prep: 30 mins** ↻   **cook: 35–40 mins** 🕙

In spite of the formidable list of ingredients, this flavorsome stew is very simple to make. It is suitable for vegetarians and vegans.

INGREDIENTS

1 red onion, sliced	2 bay leaves
2 leeks, sliced	½ tsp fennel seeds
4 garlic cloves, finely chopped	½ tsp chili powder
1 eggplant, sliced	pinch of dried thyme
1 small acorn squash, diced	pinch of dried oregano
1 small celery root, diced	pinch of sugar
2 turnips, sliced	½ cup extra virgin olive oil
2 plum tomatoes, chopped	scant 1 cup Vegetable Stock
1 carrot, sliced	(see page 13)
1 zucchini, sliced	1 oz/25 g fresh basil leaves, torn
2 red bell peppers, seeded and sliced	4 tbsp chopped fresh parsley
1 fennel bulb, sliced	salt and pepper
6 oz/175 g Swiss chard or spinach beet, chopped	2 tbsp freshly grated Parmesan cheese, to serve (optional)

NUTRITIONAL INFORMATION

Calories	307
Protein	5g
Carbohydrate	20g
Sugars	13g
Fat	24g
Saturates	3g

variation

You can use other typically Italian vegetables to make this stew, including butternut squash, cardoons, cavolo nero, pumpkin, and spinach.

cook's tip

Unless you are using pulses, nuts, or grains, it is a good idea to complement vegetable dishes with a little cheese to provide some protein.

1 Place the onion, leeks, garlic, eggplant, squash, celery root, turnips, tomatoes, carrot, zucchini, bell peppers, fennel, Swiss chard, bay leaves, fennel seeds, chili powder, thyme, oregano, sugar, olive oil, Stock, and half the torn basil leaves in a large, heavy-bottomed pan. Mix together well, then bring to a boil.

2 Reduce the heat, cover, and simmer for 30 minutes, or until tender.

3 Sprinkle in the remaining basil and the parsley and season to taste with salt and pepper. Serve immediately, sprinkled with the Parmesan cheese.

vegetable crumble

cook: 40 mins   **prep: 15 mins**   serves 4

NUTRITIONAL INFORMATION

Calories	.523
Protein	.21g
Carbohydrate	.45g
Sugars	.14g
Fat	.30g
Saturates	.13g

variation

For extra color, replace half the cauliflower with fresh green broccoli at the beginning of Step 1.

Always a family favorite, the crisp, crunchy topping of this warming crumble contrasts with the creamy mixture of vegetables, fresh herbs, and cheese sauce that lies beneath.

INGREDIENTS

1 cauliflower, cut into florets

salt and pepper

2 tbsp corn oil

2½ tbsp all-purpose flour

1½ cups milk

11½ oz/325 g canned corn kernels, drained

2 tbsp chopped fresh parsley

1 tsp chopped fresh thyme

scant 1½ cups grated Cheddar cheese

TOPPING

6 tbsp whole-wheat flour

2 tbsp butter

⅓ cup rolled oats

⅛ cup blanched almonds, chopped

cook's tip

When you make a white sauce, as in Step 1, make sure that the flour and oil mixture is smooth before adding the milk. Add the milk in small amounts to avoid forming lumps, which spoil the sauce.

1 Preheat the oven to 375°F/190°C. Cook the cauliflower in a pan of lightly salted boiling water for 5 minutes. Drain well, reserving the cooking water. Heat the oil in a pan and stir in the flour. Cook, stirring constantly, for 1 minute. Remove the pan from the heat and gradually stir in the milk and ⅔ cup of the reserved cooking water. Return the pan to the heat and bring to a boil, stirring constantly. Cook, stirring, for 3 minutes, or until thickened. Remove the pan from the heat.

2 Stir the corn, parsley, thyme, and half the cheese into the sauce and season to taste with salt and pepper. Fold in the cauliflower, then spoon the mixture into an ovenproof dish.

3 To make the crumble topping, place the flour in a bowl, add the butter, and rub it in with your fingertips until the mixture resembles bread crumbs. Stir in the oats and almonds, add the remaining cheese, then sprinkle the mixture evenly over the vegetables. Bake in the preheated oven for 30 minutes, then serve.

gratin of mixed vegetables

serves 6   **prep: 15 mins** 🕐   **cook: 1 hr 15 mins** 🕐

A topping of traditional Italian romano cheese suffuses this warming bake with a burst of extra flavor, and is a perfect complement to the hearty fresh vegetable gratin beneath.

INGREDIENTS

2 parsnips, sliced
2 tbsp olive oil
1 eggplant, diced
1 garlic clove, finely chopped
2 tsp chopped fresh thyme
salt
2 tsp butter
2 shallots, chopped
4 canned artichoke hearts, drained
4 canned celery hearts, sliced
½ cup grated Emmental cheese
½ cup freshly grated romano cheese

NUTRITIONAL INFORMATION

Calories	.150
Protein	.7g
Carbohydrate	.8g
Sugars	.4g
Fat	.12g
Saturates	.5g

cook's tip

To peel garlic, place a clove on a cutting board, lay the flat side of a cook's knife on top, press down hard and remove the skin. To release the juices, work a little salt into the clove with the flat side of the knife.

1 Preheat the oven to 350°F/180°C. Steam the parsnips over a large pan of simmering water for 4 minutes, or until just tender. Drain, then let cool.

2 Heat the oil in a heavy-bottomed skillet, then add the eggplant and cook, stirring, for 5 minutes. Add the garlic and thyme, season to taste with salt, and cook for 3 minutes. Transfer the mixture to a bowl with a perforated spoon. Melt the butter in the skillet, then add the shallots and a pinch of salt and cook over very low heat, stirring occasionally, for 7–10 minutes.

3 Mix the shallots and eggplant mixture together. Cut each artichoke heart into 8 pieces and add to the mixture with the parsnips, celery hearts, Emmental, and half the romano cheese. Mix well and spoon into an ovenproof dish, then sprinkle over the remaining romano cheese. Bake in the preheated oven for 45 minutes. Serve.

chickpea hotchpotch

cook: 2 hrs 30 mins　　**prep: 15 mins**　　　　serves 4

This is an economical, easy-to-make dish that is packed with nutritious goodness and tastes simply wonderful. It is suitable for both vegetarians and vegans.

NUTRITIONAL INFORMATION

Calories	.438
Protein	.19g
Carbohydrate	.66g
Sugars	.15g
Fat	.13g
Saturates	.2g

INGREDIENTS

8 oz/225 g dried chickpeas, soaked
overnight in enough water to cover

3 tbsp olive oil

1 large onion, sliced

2 garlic cloves, finely chopped

2 leeks, sliced

6 oz/175 g carrots, sliced

4 turnips, sliced

4 celery stalks, sliced

4 oz/115 g bulgur wheat

14 oz/400 g canned chopped tomatoes

2 tbsp snipped fresh chives, plus extra
to garnish

salt and pepper

cook's tip

When cooking the chickpeas, remember to check the water level regularly, and have boiling water to hand to top up the pan if necessary.

1 Drain the chickpeas and place in a heavy-bottomed pan. Add enough water to cover, bring to a boil, and simmer for 1½ hours.

2 Meanwhile, heat the oil in a large pan. Add the sliced onion and cook, stirring, for 5 minutes, or until softened. Add the garlic, leeks, carrots, turnips, and celery and

cook, stirring occasionally, for 5 minutes. Stir in the bulgur wheat, tomatoes, and chives, season to taste with salt and pepper, and bring to a boil. Spoon the mixture into a heatproof pudding bowl, cover with a lid of foil, and reserve.

3 When the chickpeas have been cooking for 1½ hours, set a steamer over

the pan. Place the basin inside the steamer, cover tightly, and cook for an additional 40 minutes. Remove the basin from the steamer, drain the chickpeas, then stir them into the vegetable and bulgur wheat mixture. Transfer to a warmed serving dish and serve immediately, garnished with extra chives.

vegetarian lasagna

serves 4   **prep: 20 mins, plus 30 mins soaking**   **cook: 40 mins**

Layers of pasta, tomatoes, and mushrooms are baked in a creamy sauce for a filling, colorful, and truly scrumptious supper. It is best served with salad and crusty bread.

INGREDIENTS

1½ oz/40 g dried porcini mushrooms

2 tbsp olive oil

1 onion, finely chopped

14 oz/400 g canned chopped tomatoes

salt and pepper

¼ cup butter, plus extra for greasing

1 lb/450 g white mushrooms, thinly sliced

1 garlic clove, finely chopped

1 tbsp lemon juice

½ tsp Dijon mustard

¾ quantity Cheese Sauce (see page 90), made with Cheddar cheese

6 sheets no-precook lasagna

½ cup freshly grated Parmesan cheese

NUTRITIONAL INFORMATION

Calories 628

Protein 24g

Carbohydrate 43g

Sugars 11g

Fat 41g

Saturates 23g

variation

You can replace the freshly grated Parmesan cheese with grated Cheddar cheese in Step 3, if you prefer.

cook's tip

Instead of grating the Parmesan cheese, you can shave off very thin strips using a vegetable peeler, to give a different consistency to the topping.

1 Preheat the oven to 400°F/200°C. Place the porcini mushrooms in a small bowl, cover with boiling water, and let soak for 30 minutes. Meanwhile, heat the oil in a small skillet. Add the chopped onion and cook, stirring occasionally, for 5 minutes, or until softened. Add the tomatoes and cook, stirring frequently, for 7–8 minutes. Season with salt and pepper and reserve.

2 Drain and slice the porcini mushrooms. Melt half the butter in a large, heavy-bottomed skillet. Add the porcini and white mushrooms and cook until they begin to release their juices. Add the garlic and lemon juice and season to taste with salt and pepper. Cook over low heat, stirring occasionally, until almost all the liquid has evaporated.

3 Lightly grease an ovenproof dish with butter. Stir the mustard into the Cheese Sauce, then spread a layer over the bottom of the dish. Place a layer of lasagna sheets on top, cover with the mushrooms, another layer of sauce, another layer of lasagna, the tomato mixture, and finally, another layer of sauce. Sprinkle with the Parmesan cheese and dot with the remaining butter. Bake in the preheated oven for 20 minutes. Let stand for 5 minutes before serving.

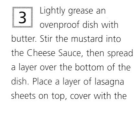

artichoke heart soufflé

serves 4 | **prep: 20 mins** | **cook: 40 mins**

This exquisite, impressive dish is perfect for entertaining, but to guarantee maximum impact, be sure to serve it as soon as the dish comes out of the oven.

INGREDIENTS

¼ cup butter, plus extra
for greasing

6 tbsp all-purpose flour

1¼ cups milk

pinch of freshly grated nutmeg

salt and pepper

2 tbsp light cream

½ cup grated Emmental cheese

6 canned artichoke hearts,
drained and mashed

4 egg yolks

5 egg whites

NUTRITIONAL INFORMATION

Calories 350

Protein 18g

Carbohydrate 18g

Sugars 6g

Fat 24g

Saturates 13g

variation

For a spinach soufflé, substitute 8 oz/225 g of cooked, drained, and chopped spinach for the artichoke hearts.

1 Preheat the oven to 375°F/190°C. Grease a 7-cup soufflé dish with butter, then tie a double strip of waxed paper around the dish so that it protrudes about 2 inches/5 cm above the rim.

2 Melt the butter in a large, heavy-bottomed pan. Add the flour and cook, stirring constantly, for 2 minutes. Remove from the heat and gradually stir in the milk. Return to the heat and bring to a boil, whisking constantly, for 2 minutes, or until thickened and smooth. Remove from the heat, season with nutmeg, salt, and pepper, then beat in the cream, cheese, and artichoke hearts. Beat in the egg yolks, 1 at a time.

3 Whisk the egg whites in a grease-free bowl until they form stiff peaks. Fold 2 tablespoons of the egg whites into the artichoke mixture to loosen, then gently fold in the remainder.

4 Carefully pour the mixture into the prepared soufflé dish and bake in the preheated oven for 35 minutes, or until the soufflé is well risen and the top is golden. Serve immediately.

lentil, shallot & mushroom pie

🕙 cook: 1 hr 30 mins   🕙 prep: 25 mins, plus 45 mins   serves 6
cooling and chilling

*This makes a great dish for a dinner party main meal, as it is rich in
texture, tasty, and filling, and the scrunched phyllo pastry topping
looks hugely appetizing and attractive.*

NUTRITIONAL INFORMATION

Calories	.439
Protein	.18g
Carbohydrate	.75g
Sugars	.2g
Fat	.9g
Saturates	.4g

INGREDIENTS

scant 1 cup Puy or green lentils

2 bay leaves

6 shallots, sliced

5 cups Vegetable Stock
(see page 13)

salt and pepper

¼ cup butter

generous 1 cup long-grain rice

8 sheets phyllo pastry, thawed if frozen

2 tbsp chopped fresh parsley

2 tsp chopped fresh fennel or savory

4 eggs, 1 beaten and 3 hard-cooked
and sliced

8 oz/225 g portobello mushrooms

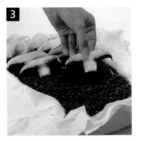

cook's tip

Make sure that you allow the
lentils and rice mixture to cool
before layering them inside
the pastry, because the pie has
to be chilled in the refrigerator
before cooking.

1 Preheat the oven
to 375°F/190°C. Put
the lentils, bay leaves, and half
the shallots into a large, heavy-
bottomed pan. Add half the
Stock, bring to a boil, and
simmer for 25 minutes, or until
the lentils are tender. Remove
from the heat, season to taste
with salt and pepper, and let
cool completely.

2 Melt half the butter in
a heavy-bottomed pan,
then add the remaining
shallots and cook, stirring
occasionally, for 5 minutes, or
until softened. Stir in the rice
and cook, stirring constantly,
for 1 minute, then add the
remaining Stock. Season to
taste with salt and pepper and
bring to a boil. Reduce the
heat, then cover and simmer

for 15 minutes. Remove the
pan from the heat and let
cool completely.

3 Melt the remaining
butter over low heat,
then brush an ovenproof dish
with a little of it. Arrange the
phyllo sheets in the dish with
the sides overhanging (these
will make the pie lid), brushing
each sheet with melted butter.

Add the parsley and fennel to
the rice mixture, then beat in
the beaten egg. Make layers of
rice, hard-cooked egg, lentils,
and mushrooms in the dish,
seasoning each layer. Bring up
the phyllo sheets and scrunch
into folds on top. Brush with
melted butter and chill for
15 minutes. Bake in the oven
for 45 minutes. Let stand for
10 minutes before serving.

vegetarian moussaka

cook: 1 hour   **prep: 30 mins**   **serves 4**

NUTRITIONAL INFORMATION

Calories 490

Protein 18g

Carbohydrate 27g

Sugars 11g

Fat 35g

Saturates 11g

variation

For the traditional meat-eaters' version of this dish, substitute 12 oz/350 g minced lamb for the lentils. Brown with the onions for 10 minutes.

This version of the popular Greek dish is made with green lentils rather than minced lamb, but it is still topped with a traditional layer of fried eggplants and a little Parmesan cheese.

INGREDIENTS

about ½ cup olive oil

1 onion, chopped

4 celery stalks, chopped

1 garlic clove, finely chopped

14 oz/400 g canned chopped tomatoes

10½ oz/300 g canned green lentils

2 tbsp chopped fresh parsley

salt and pepper

1 large eggplant, sliced

TOPPING

2 tbsp butter

2½ tbsp all-purpose flour

1¼ cups milk

pinch of freshly grated nutmeg

1 egg

½ cup freshly grated Parmesan cheese

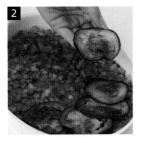

cook's tip

To prevent the eggplant from absorbing too much oil during cooking, salt it first. Place the slices in a colander, sprinkle over some salt, and let stand for 20 minutes to let them dry out.

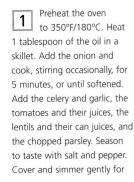

1 Preheat the oven to 350°F/180°C. Heat 1 tablespoon of the oil in a skillet. Add the onion and cook, stirring occasionally, for 5 minutes, or until softened. Add the celery and garlic, the tomatoes and their juices, the lentils and their can juices, and the chopped parsley. Season to taste with salt and pepper. Cover and simmer gently for 15 minutes, or until the mixture has thickened.

2 Meanwhile, heat a little of the remaining oil in a large, heavy-bottomed skillet. Add the eggplant slices, in batches, if necessary, and cook until golden on both sides, adding more oil as necessary. Remove from the skillet and drain on paper towels. Layer an ovenproof dish with the lentil and tomato mixture and the eggplant slices, ending with a layer of eggplant.

3 To make the topping, put the butter, flour, and milk into a pan and bring to a boil over low heat, whisking constantly. Season to taste with nutmeg, salt, and pepper. Remove the pan from the heat, let cool slightly, then beat in the egg. Pour the sauce over the eggplants, sprinkle with the Parmesan cheese, and bake in the preheated oven for 30–40 minutes, or until golden.

vegetable & bean curd strudels

serves 4   **prep: 25 mins**   **cook: 30 mins**

These strudels look really impressive and are perfect if friends are coming round or for a more formal dinner party dish.

INGREDIENTS

8 oz/225 g firm bean curd
(drained weight)

2 tbsp vegetable oil

4 tbsp butter

scant 1 cup diced potatoes

1 leek, shredded

2 garlic cloves, crushed

1 tsp garam masala

½ tsp chili powder

½ tsp turmeric

1¾ oz/50 g okra, sliced

3½ oz/100 g mushrooms, sliced

2 tomatoes, diced

salt and pepper

12 sheets phyllo pastry

NUTRITIONAL INFORMATION

Calories 485

Protein 16g

Carbohydrate 47g

Sugars 5g

Fat 27g

Saturates 5g

variation

For a slightly stronger flavor, and to add a little crunchiness in the texture, try substituting a bunch of scallions, chopped, for the leek.

1 Preheat the oven to 375°F/190°C. Cut the bean curd into dice and reserve. Heat the oil and half the butter in a large, heavy-bottomed skillet. Add the potatoes and leek and cook, stirring constantly, for 2–3 minutes. Add the garlic and spices, okra, mushrooms, tomatoes, and bean curd, then season to taste with salt and pepper. Cook, stirring constantly, for 5–7 minutes, or until tender.

2 Melt the remaining butter in a small pan over low heat. Lay the pastry out on a cutting board and brush each individual sheet with a little melted butter. Place 3 sheets on top of one another, then repeat to make 4 stacks. Spoon one fourth of the filling along the center of each stack and brush the edges with a little melted butter. Fold the short edges in and roll up lengthwise to form a cigar shape. Brush the outside of the strudels with melted butter. Brush a cookie sheet with a little melted butter and place the strudels on it.

3 Cook in the preheated oven for 20 minutes, or until golden brown and crisp. Transfer to a warmed serving dish and serve immediately.

phyllo pockets

cook: 45 mins

prep: 20 mins, plus 1 hr cooling/chilling

serves 6

These crisp pastry pockets can be served as a main course with a potato salad and salad greens or on their own as appetizers.

NUTRITIONAL INFORMATION

Calories	.410
Protein	.14g
Carbohydrate	.45g
Sugars	.4g
Fat	.19g
Saturates	.11g

INGREDIENTS

4 tbsp butter

1 tbsp corn oil

4 leeks, sliced

2 onions, chopped

1 garlic clove, finely chopped

2 tsp chopped fresh thyme

salt and pepper

2 tbsp light cream

scant 1½ cups grated Swiss or Emmental cheese

12 sheets phyllo pastry

cook's tip

Try decorating the outside of these vegetable pockets with crumpled pieces of phyllo pastry before cooking for a really impressive effect.

1 Preheat the oven to 350°F/180°C. Melt half the butter with the oil in a large, heavy-bottomed skillet over low heat. Add the leeks, onions, garlic, and thyme and season to taste. Cook, stirring frequently, for 10 minutes. Stir in the cream and cook for an additional 2–3 minutes, or until the liquid has been absorbed. Remove the skillet from the heat and let cool. Stir in the cheese, cover with plastic wrap, and chill in the refrigerator for 30 minutes.

2 Melt the remaining butter and brush a little on to a cookie sheet. Brush 2 sheets of phyllo with butter and place them one on top of the other. Place a heaped spoonful of the leek mixture close to 1 corner. Fold the corner over the filling, then fold in the sides and roll up the pocket. Place the pocket, seam-side down, on the cookie sheet and make 5 more pockets in the same way.

3 Brush the phyllo pockets with the remaining melted butter and bake in the preheated oven for 30 minutes, or until crisp and golden. Serve immediately.

mushroom gougère

serves 4

prep: 20 mins, plus 10 mins cooling

cook: 1 hr

A gougère is a delicious savory circle of light choux pastry, usually flavored with cheese. It can be served warm or cold, making it ideal for preparing an evening meal in advance.

INGREDIENTS

CHOUX PASTRY

½ cup white bread flour

pinch of salt

¼ cup butter, plus extra for greasing

⅔ cup water

2 eggs

½ cup grated Emmental cheese

FILLING

2 tbsp olive oil

1 onion, chopped

8 oz/225 g cremini mushrooms, sliced

2 garlic cloves, finely chopped

1 tbsp all-purpose flour

⅔ cup Vegetable Stock (see page 13)

¾ cup chopped walnuts

2 tbsp chopped fresh parsley

salt and pepper

NUTRITIONAL INFORMATION

Calories 490

Protein 14g

Carbohydrate 21g

Sugars 3g

Fat 39g

Saturates 13g

variation

If you want to use up a carton of white mushrooms, as long as they still feel firm, they will work just as well as the cremini mushrooms.

cook's tip

When making the choux pastry, make sure that the flour is nearby so you can quickly tip it into the mixture in a single movement at the correct moment, otherwise the pastry may be spoiled.

1 Preheat the oven to 400°F/200°C. To make the pastry, sift the flour and salt on to a sheet of waxed paper. Heat the butter and water in a pan until the butter melts, but do not let it boil. Add the flour all at once and beat vigorously with a wooden spoon until the mixture is smooth and comes away from the sides of the pan. Remove from the heat, cool for 10 minutes, then gradually beat in the eggs until smooth and glossy. Beat in the cheese. Grease a round ovenproof dish with butter and spoon the pastry dough around the sides.

2 To make the filling, heat the olive oil in a large, heavy-bottomed skillet. Add the onion and cook, stirring occasionally, for 5 minutes, or until softened. Add the mushrooms and garlic and cook for 2 minutes. Stir in the flour and cook, stirring, for 1 minute, then gradually stir in the Stock. Bring to a boil, stirring, and cook for 3 minutes, or until thickened. Reserve 2 tablespoons of the walnuts and stir the remainder into the mushroom mixture with the parsley. Season to taste with salt and pepper.

3 Spoon the mushroom filling into the center of the dish and sprinkle the reserved walnuts over it. Bake in the preheated oven for about 40 minutes, or until risen and golden. Serve immediately.

mediterranean crêpes

cook: 1 hr 15 mins   **prep: 25 mins**   **serves 4**

A rich tomato and herb filling makes these delicious crêpes completely irresistible. Serve with crisp, leafy salad greens or with a side dish of Peas with Pearl Onions (see page 176).

INGREDIENTS

1 tbsp corn oil, plus extra for brushing

1 quantity Crêpe Batter (see page 13)

FILLING

2 tbsp olive oil

1 onion, chopped

2 garlic cloves, finely chopped

1 small eggplant, diced

1 red bell pepper, seeded and diced

4 tomatoes, peeled and diced

1 tbsp sun-dried tomato paste

1 tbsp chopped fresh parsley

2 tsp chopped fresh thyme

salt and pepper

TOPPING

2 tbsp butter, melted

3 tbsp freshly grated Parmesan cheese

variation

Substitute chopped fresh oregano and basil for the parsley and thyme for a slightly different flavor.

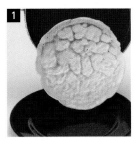

cook's tip

The secret to making successful crêpes is to make sure that the oil is very hot before pouring the batter into a good-quality non-stick pan.

1 Preheat the oven to 375°F/190°C. Brush a crêpe pan with oil and heat well. Add a little batter and quickly tilt and rotate the pan to cover the bottom with a thin layer. Cook for 1 minute, or until the underside is golden. Flip over with a spatula and cook the second side for 30 seconds, until golden. Slide the crêpe out on to a plate. Cook the remaining batter in the same way to make 12 crêpes, stacking them on the plate interleaved with waxed paper. Keep warm.

2 To make the filling, heat the oil in a heavy-bottomed skillet. Add the onion and cook, stirring occasionally, for 5 minutes, or until softened. Add the garlic, eggplant and red bell pepper and cook, stirring occasionally, for 10 minutes. Stir in the tomatoes, sun-dried tomato paste, parsley, and thyme. Season to taste with salt and pepper, cover, and simmer for 15 minutes. Lightly brush an ovenproof dish with oil. Divide the filling between the crêpes, roll up, and place in the dish, seam-side down.

3 Brush the crêpes with melted butter, sprinkle with the Parmesan cheese, and bake in the preheated oven for 15 minutes. Serve immediately.

spinach & cheese crêpes

serves 4   **prep: 25 mins** ⏱   **cook: 45 mins** ⏱

Ricotta cheese and spinach are made for each other and feature in many Italian recipes. Here they are combined in a delicious filling for crêpes, which are then baked in a creamy sauce in the oven.

INGREDIENTS

1 tbsp corn oil, plus
extra for brushing

1 quantity Crêpe Batter
(see page 13)

½ quantity hot Cheese Sauce
(see page 90), made
with Parmesan cheese

4 oz/115 g mozzarella cheese,
thinly sliced

FILLING

1 lb 10 oz/750 g fresh spinach,
coarse stems removed

2 tbsp butter

8 oz/225 g ricotta cheese

1 egg, lightly beaten

pinch of freshly grated nutmeg

salt and pepper

NUTRITIONAL INFORMATION

Calories	.630
Protein	.36g
Carbohydrate	.38g
Sugars	.12g
Fat	.38g
Saturates	.20g

variation

If you like, substitute buckwheat flour for half the all-purpose flour when making the crêpe batter.

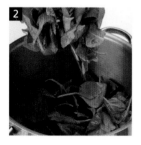

cook's tip

Make sure you remove as much water as possible when you drain the spinach, otherwise the excess moisture may make the crêpes soggy.

1 Preheat the oven to 425°F/220°C. Brush a crêpe pan with oil and heat well. Add a little Batter and quickly tilt and rotate the pan to cover the bottom with a thin layer. Cook for 1 minute, or until the underside is golden. Flip over with a spatula and cook the second side for about 30 seconds, until golden. Slide the crêpe

out on to a plate. Cook the remaining Batter in the same way to make 12 crêpes, stacking them on the plate interleaved with waxed paper. Keep warm.

2 To make the filling, put the spinach into a heavy-bottomed pan with just the water clinging to the leaves after washing, then cook for

7 minutes. Drain thoroughly and squeeze out any excess moisture. Chop the spinach coarsely, place in a blender or food processor with the butter, and process to a smooth paste. Add the ricotta cheese and process until blended. Scrape into a bowl, stir in the egg, and season to taste with nutmeg, salt, and pepper. Brush an ovenproof

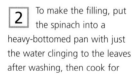

dish with a little oil. Divide the spinach mixture between the crêpes, then roll up and place in the dish, seam-side down.

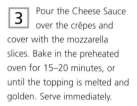

3 Pour the Cheese Sauce over the crêpes and cover with the mozzarella slices. Bake in the preheated oven for 15–20 minutes, or until the topping is melted and golden. Serve immediately.

potato-topped lentil bake

⏲ **cook: 1 hr 30 mins**   ⏱ **prep: 10 mins**   **serves 4**

A wonderful mixture of red lentils, bean curd, and vegetables is cooked beneath a crunchy potato topping for a really hearty meal. It is best served with fresh salad greens.

variation

This dish is very adaptable—you can use almost any combination of your favorite vegetables to make it.

INGREDIENTS

generous 1 cup red split lentils

4 tbsp butter

1 leek, sliced

2 garlic cloves, crushed

1 celery stalk, chopped

4½ oz/125 g broccoli florets

6 oz/175 g smoked bean curd, cubed

(drained weight)

2 tsp tomato paste

salt and pepper

fresh thyme sprigs, to garnish

TOPPING

1 lb 8 oz/675 g floury potatoes, diced

2 tbsp butter

1 tbsp milk

⅓ cup chopped pecans

2 tbsp chopped fresh thyme

cook's tip

Do not let the potatoes overcook in Step 1, otherwise they will lose their firmness and the mash topping may turn out thin and slightly soggy.

1 Preheat the oven to 400°F/200°C. To make the topping, cook the potatoes in a large pan of boiling water for 10–15 minutes, or until cooked through. Drain well and transfer to a bowl. Add the butter and milk to the bowl and mash thoroughly. Stir in the chopped pecans and chopped fresh thyme and reserve.

2 Place the lentils in a large pan of boiling water and cook for 20–30 minutes, or until tender. Drain and reserve. Melt the butter in a large skillet. Add the leek, garlic, celery, and broccoli. Cook, stirring frequently, for 5 minutes, or until softened. Add the bean curd cubes. Stir in the lentils and tomato paste. Season to taste with salt and pepper, then transfer the mixture to a shallow ovenproof dish.

3 Spoon the potato topping on top of the lentil mixture, spreading to cover. Cook in the preheated oven for 30–35 minutes, or until the topping is golden. Garnish with fresh thyme sprigs and serve immediately.

bean burgers

serves 4   prep: 15 mins ◔   cook: 20 mins

These tasty veggie burgers are not only much more delicious than the ready-made varieties, they are more nutritious, too—which is good news if you are cooking for children. This recipe is suitable for both vegetarians and vegans.

INGREDIENTS

1 tbsp corn oil, plus	15 oz/425 g canned pinto or red
extra for brushing	kidney beans, drained and rinsed
1 onion, finely chopped	2 tbsp chopped fresh
1 garlic clove, finely chopped	flatleaf parsley
1 tsp ground coriander	salt and pepper
1 tsp ground cumin	all-purpose flour, for dusting
4 oz/115 g white mushrooms,	bread rolls and salad greens,
finely chopped	to serve

NUTRITIONAL INFORMATION

Calories 145

Protein 8g

Carbohydrate 20g

Sugars 6g

Fat 4g

Saturates 1g

variation

For more colorful burgers, you can substitute 4 oz/115 g of mixed, finely chopped zucchini and carrot for the mushrooms.

cook's tip

If the burgers do not hold together when you try to shape them, add just a little more oil to the mixture to make them easier to handle.

1 Heat the oil in a heavy-bottomed skillet. Add the onion and cook, stirring occasionally, for 5 minutes, or until softened. Add the garlic, coriander, and cumin and cook, stirring frequently, for an additional 1 minute. Add the mushrooms and cook, stirring constantly, for 4–5 minutes, or until all the liquid has evaporated. Transfer to a bowl.

2 Place the beans in a small bowl and mash with a potato masher or fork. Stir the beans into the mushroom mixture with the parsley, and season to taste with salt and pepper.

3 Divide the mixture into 4 portions, dip in a little flour and shape into flat, round patties. Brush with oil and cook under a preheated medium–hot broiler for 4–5 minutes on each side. Serve in bread rolls with salad greens.

tomato soufflés

serves 4 **prep: 20 mins, plus 10 mins cooling** **cook: 30 mins**

These individual soufflés are cooked in an ingenious way—they puff out from succulent tomato shells, making an intriguing and attractive dish. They work well as a dinner party appetizer.

INGREDIENTS

6 beefsteak tomatoes, halved

2 tbsp butter

2½ tbsp all-purpose flour

2 tbsp heavy cream

2 tbsp freshly grated Parmesan cheese

½ tsp mustard powder

pinch of freshly grated nutmeg

salt and pepper

5 egg whites

4 egg yolks

NUTRITIONAL INFORMATION

Calories	179
Protein	. . . . .7g
Carbohydrate	. . . . .8g
Sugars	. . . . .5g
Fat	. . . . .13g
Saturates	. . . . .7g

cook's tip

If the tomato shells still look moist after draining, pat them dry with paper towels before spooning in the soufflé mixture, so that the finished soufflés sit firmly in place.

1 Preheat the oven to 425°F/220°C. Scoop out the flesh and seeds of the tomatoes with a teaspoon and reserve. Place the shells upside down on paper towels to drain. Place the flesh and seeds in a pan and simmer gently for 3 minutes. Rub the warmed mixture through a fine strainer into a small bowl and reserve.

2 Melt the butter in a small pan over a low heat. Stir in the flour and cook, stirring constantly, for 1 minute. Remove the pan from the heat and gradually stir in the reserved tomato and the cream. Return the pan to the heat and cook, stirring constantly, for 2 minutes, or until smooth and thickened. Remove the pan from the heat, stir in the Parmesan cheese and mustard powder, and season to taste with nutmeg, salt, and pepper. Let cool for 10 minutes.

3 Whisk the egg whites in a clean, grease-free bowl until they form stiff peaks. Beat the egg yolks into the tomato mixture, 1 at a time. Fold 2 tablespoons of the egg whites into the mixture, then gently fold in the remainder. Divide the soufflé mixture between them. Place on a cookie sheet and bake in the preheated oven for 5 minutes. Reduce the oven temperature to 400°F/200°C and bake for an additional 15–20 minutes, or until golden. Serve immediately.

kidney bean kiev

cook: 20 mins

prep: 25 mins, plus 10 mins cooling

serves 4

This is a vegetarian version of chicken Kiev—the bean patties are molded around garlic and herb butter, coated in bread crumbs, and sautéed until golden brown. Serve with salad, if you like.

NUTRITIONAL INFORMATION

Calories	.688
Protein	.17g
Carbohydrate	.49g
Sugars	.8g
Fat	.49g
Saturates	.20g

INGREDIENTS

generous ½ cup butter

3 garlic cloves, crushed

2 tbsp chopped fresh parsley

1 lb 8 oz/675 g canned red kidney beans

3 cups fresh white bread crumbs

1 leek, chopped

1 celery stalk, chopped

salt and pepper

1 egg, beaten

2 tbsp vegetable oil

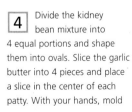

1 Place the garlic and 1 tablespoon of parsley in a large bowl with all but 2 tablespoons of the butter and blend together with a wooden spoon. Transfer the garlic butter on to a sheet of parchment paper, roll into a cigar shape, and wrap in the parchment paper. Chill in the refrigerator until required.

2 Using a potato masher, mash the red kidney beans in a large bowl and stir in 1½ cups bread crumbs until thoroughly blended.

3 Melt the remaining butter in a large skillet. Add the leek and celery and sauté, stirring constantly, for 3–4 minutes. Add the bean mixture and the remaining parsley. Season to taste with salt and pepper and mix well. Remove from the heat and let cool slightly.

4 Divide the kidney bean mixture into 4 equal portions and shape them into ovals. Slice the garlic butter into 4 pieces and place a slice in the center of each patty. With your hands, mold the bean mixture around the garlic butter to encase it completely. Dip each bean patty into the beaten egg to coat, then roll in the remaining bread crumbs.

5 Heat the oil in a separate large skillet and cook the patties, turning once, for 7–10 minutes, or until golden. Serve immediately.

variation

Use other canned beans, such as flageolet beans, and use chopped fresh cilantro instead of parsley, if you prefer.

glamorgan sausages with yam mash

🍲 cook: 40 mins　　　🕐 prep: 30 mins　　　serves 4

NUTRITIONAL INFORMATION

Calories 909

Protein 21g

Carbohydrate 63g

Sugars 14g

Fat 65g

Saturates 36g

variation

For a slightly different flavor, try substituting a few finely chopped scallions for the leek.

Bangers and mash may well be a favorite supper among meat-eaters, but this more sophisticated vegetarian version is far superior in flavor and much healthier.

INGREDIENTS

SAUSAGES	MASH
generous 2 cups fresh whole-wheat bread crumbs	1 lb 9 oz/700 g yams (dark sweet potatoes), unpeeled
scant 2 cups grated Caerphilly cheese	salt and pepper
1 leek, finely chopped	½ cup butter
2 tbsp finely chopped fresh parsley	1 onion, grated
1 tbsp finely chopped fresh marjoram	½ cup heavy cream
1 tbsp whole-grain mustard	pinch of freshly grated nutmeg
2 eggs	
pepper	
corn oil, for deep-frying	
generous ⅓ cup dried bread crumbs	

cook's tip

If you are making your own fresh bread crumbs, weigh the bread in slices to find the correct amount, then break the slices into smaller pieces, place in a food processor and process in short bursts.

1 For the mash, cook the yams in a large pan of lightly salted boiling water for 25–30 minutes, or until tender. Meanwhile, begin making the sausages. Mix the fresh bread crumbs, cheese, leek, parsley, marjoram, and mustard in a bowl. Separate 1 egg, reserve the white, and add the yolk with the remaining whole egg to the mixture. Season to taste with pepper and knead lightly until the mixture comes together. Using your fingers, form it into 8 sausage shapes.

2 When the potatoes are tender, drain and let cool slightly, then peel and mash with a potato masher. Heat the butter in a small skillet over very low heat. Add the onion and stir-fry for 5 minutes. Pour the onion mixture into the mashed potatoes, add the cream, and beat with a wooden spoon. Season to taste with nutmeg, salt, and pepper. Keep warm.

3 Heat the oil for deep-frying to 350–375°F/ 180–190°C, or until a cube of bread browns in 30 seconds. Meanwhile, whisk the reserved egg white in a shallow dish until frothy. Place the dried bread crumbs in a separate dish. Dip the sausages in the egg white, then in the bread crumbs to coat. Deep-fry the sausages, in batches, for 2 minutes. Drain on paper towels and keep warm while you cook the remainder. Serve immediately with the yam mash.

lentil roast

serves 6   **prep: 15 mins**   **cook: 1 hr 20 mins**

This is the perfect dish to serve for a vegetarian Sunday lunch. Roasted vegetables make a succulent accompaniment.

INGREDIENTS

generous 1 cup red split lentils

2 cups Vegetable Stock

(see page 13)

1 bay leaf

1 tbsp butter or vegetarian

margarine, softened

2 tbsp dried whole-wheat

bread crumbs

generous 2 cups grated mature

Cheddar cheese

1 leek, finely chopped

4½ oz/125 g white mushrooms,

finely chopped

1⅔ cups fresh whole-wheat

bread crumbs

2 tbsp chopped fresh parsley

1 tbsp lemon juice

2 eggs, lightly beaten

salt and pepper

fresh flatleaf parsley sprigs,

to garnish

mixed roasted vegetables, to serve

NUTRITIONAL INFORMATION	
Calories 600	
Protein 26g	
Carbohydrate 32g	
Sugars 2g	
Fat 20g	
Saturates 10g	

variation

Substitute another chopped fresh herb of your choice for the parsley in Step 3, if you prefer.

cook's tip

When you spoon the lentil mixture into the loaf pan, make sure that you push it into the corners of the pan, otherwise the finished roasted loaf will lose its shape.

1 Preheat the oven to 375°F/190°C. Place the lentils, Stock, and bay leaf in a large, heavy-bottomed pan. Bring to a boil, cover, and simmer for 15–20 minutes, or until all of the liquid is absorbed. Remove and discard the bay leaf.

2 Line the bottom of a 2 lb 4-oz/1-kg loaf pan with parchment paper. Grease the pan and lining with the butter and sprinkle over the dried bread crumbs.

3 Stir the cheese, leek, mushrooms, fresh bread crumbs, and parsley into the lentils. Bind the mixture together with the lemon juice and beaten eggs. Season to taste with salt and pepper.

Spoon into the prepared loaf pan and smooth the top. Bake in the preheated oven for 1 hour, or until golden. Loosen the loaf with a spatula and turn out on to a warmed serving plate. Garnish with parsley and serve sliced, with roasted vegetables.

vegetable & hazelnut loaf

serves 4   **prep: 30 mins** ⟲   **cook: 1 hr 15 mins** ⟳

Serve this flavorsome loaf hot with Potato Fans (see page 161) and Tomato Sauce (see page 83) or cold with Fruity Coleslaw (see page 200) and salad greens. It is suitable for vegetarians and vegans.

INGREDIENTS

2 tbsp corn oil, plus extra for greasing

1 onion, chopped

1 garlic clove, finely chopped

2 celery stalks, chopped

1 tbsp all-purpose flour

generous ¾ cup strained tomatoes

generous 2 cups fresh whole-wheat bread crumbs

2 carrots, grated

1 cup ground toasted hazelnuts

1 tbsp dark soy sauce

2 tbsp chopped fresh cilantro

1 egg, lightly beaten

salt and pepper

NUTRITIONAL INFORMATION	
Calories	.369
Protein	.10g
Carbohydrate	.25g
Sugars	.7g
Fat	.26g
Saturates	.3g

variation

You can cook the loaf in a round cake pan and serve in wedges for a different presentation, if you like.

1 Preheat the oven to 350°C/180°C. Heat the oil in a heavy-bottomed skillet. Add the onion and cook, stirring occasionally, for 5 minutes, or until softened. Add the garlic and celery and cook, stirring frequently, for 5 minutes. Add the flour and cook, stirring constantly, for 1 minute. Gradually stir in the strained tomatoes and cook, stirring constantly, until thickened. Remove the skillet from the heat.

2 Put the bread crumbs, carrots, toasted hazelnuts, soy sauce, and cilantro into a bowl. Add the tomato mixture and stir well. Let cool slightly, then beat in the egg and season to taste with salt and pepper.

3 Grease and line a 1-lb/450-g loaf pan. Spoon the mixture into the pan and smooth the surface. Cover with foil and bake in the preheated oven for 1 hour. If serving hot, turn the loaf out on to a warmed serving dish and serve immediately. Alternatively, let cool in the pan before turning out.

risotto alla rustica

cook: 30 minutes   **prep: 5 mins**   **serves 4**

A proper risotto is a delicious dish, but it cannot be hurried. It is essential to add the liquid gradually, allowing each addition to be fully absorbed before adding the next, to produce the right texture.

NUTRITIONAL INFORMATION

Calories	.519
Protein	.8g
Carbohydrate	.89g
Sugars	.6g
Fat	.16g
Saturates	.7g

INGREDIENTS

scant 3½ cups Vegetable Stock (see page 13)

3 tbsp butter

2 tbsp olive oil

1 onion, finely chopped

2 shallots, finely chopped

1 garlic clove, finely chopped

1¾ cups risotto rice

scant ¼ cup dry white wine

4 plum tomatoes, peeled

1 fresh rosemary sprig, chopped

1 tbsp chopped fresh parsley

4 fresh basil leaves, torn

salt and pepper

2 tbsp light cream

cook's tip

Unlike other rice dishes, risotto needs to be stirred almost constantly to ensure that the rice grains absorb as much stock as possible.

1 Pour the Vegetable Stock into a large pan, bring to a boil, reduce the heat to a simmer, and keep hot.

2 Meanwhile, melt 2 tablespoons of the butter with the oil in a large pan over low heat. Add the onion, shallots, and garlic and cook, stirring occasionally, for 5 minutes.

3 Add the risotto rice to the onion mixture and stir for about 1 minute to the coat the grains with the butter and olive oil. Pour in the dry white wine, bring to a boil, and cook, stirring, until almost all the liquid has evaporated. Add the plum tomatoes, breaking them up with a fork, then add the fresh rosemary, parsley, and basil.

4 Add the hot Vegetable Stock, a large ladleful at a time, stirring until each addition is absorbed into the rice. Continue adding stock in this way, cooking until the rice is creamy, but the grains are still firm. This will take about 20 minutes. Stir in the remaining butter and season to taste with salt and pepper. Stir in the cream and serve.

vegetable biryani

cook: 1 hr

prep: 15 mins, plus 2 hrs marinating

serves 4

variation

If okra is unavailable, then use the same amount of string beans, sliced in half, and use cremini mushrooms instead of the white ones.

The biryani originated in the north of India, and was a dish reserved for festivals. Traditionally, lamb or chicken are used, but in this vegetarian version, fresh vegetables marinated in a delicious yogurt dressing are the ideal substitute for meat.

INGREDIENTS

1 large potato, cubed	1 tbsp grated fresh gingerroot
3½ oz/100 g baby carrots	2 large onions, grated
1¾ oz/50 g okra, thickly sliced	4 garlic cloves, crushed
salt	1 tsp ground turmeric
2 celery stalks, sliced	1 tbsp curry powder
2¾ oz/75 g baby white mushrooms, halved	generous 1 cup basmati rice
1 eggplant, halved and sliced	2 tbsp butter
	2 onions, sliced
1¼ cups plain yogurt	fresh cilantro leaves, to garnish

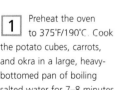

cook's tip

Basmati rice can be soaked before cooking to give a softer grain. For soaking advice and times, check the package instructions before cooking.

1 Preheat the oven to 375°F/190°C. Cook the potato cubes, carrots, and okra in a large, heavy-bottomed pan of boiling salted water for 7–8 minutes. Drain and place in a bowl. Mix with the celery, mushrooms, and eggplant.

2 Mix the yogurt, gingerroot, onions, garlic, turmeric, and curry powder and spoon over the vegetables. Let marinate in a cool place for 2 hours. Cook the rice in a large pan of boiling water for 7 minutes. Drain and reserve.

3 Heat the butter in a large skillet over medium heat. Add the onions and cook for 5–6 minutes, or until golden. Remove a few from the skillet and reserve.

4 Add the marinated vegetables to the onions in the skillet and cook for 10 minutes. Place half the basmati rice in an 8-cup casserole dish and spoon the cooked vegetables over the top. Cover with the remaining rice. Cover and cook in the preheated oven for 20–25 minutes, or until the rice is tender.

5 Spoon the biryani on to a large serving plate, garnish with the reserved onions and cilantro leaves, and serve immediately.

vegetarian paella

serves 6　　　　　**prep: 15 mins**　　　　　**cook: 40 mins**

Contrary to popular belief, paella does not invariably contain shellfish. In fact, there are many different recipes for this popular Spanish dish. This dish is suitable for vegetarians and vegans.

INGREDIENTS

¼ tsp saffron threads

6 tbsp olive oil

1 Spanish onion, sliced

3 garlic cloves, finely chopped

1 red bell pepper, seeded and sliced

1 orange bell pepper, seeded and sliced

1 large eggplant, cut into cubes

generous 1 cup risotto rice

2½ cups Vegetable Stock (see page 13)

1 lb/450 g tomatoes, peeled and chopped

salt and pepper

4 oz/115 g mushrooms, sliced

4 oz/115 g green beans, halved

14 oz/400 g canned pinto beans

NUTRITIONAL INFORMATION

Calories 359

Protein 10g

Carbohydrate 52g

Sugars 8g

Fat 14g

Saturates 2g

cook's tip

Risotto rice is rounder than long-grain rice and can absorb a lot of liquid without becoming soggy. Spanish rice, which would be more authentic in this dish, is similar but is not so widely available.

1 Place the saffron and 3 tablespoons of hot water in a bowl and reserve. Meanwhile, heat the oil in a large skillet or paella pan. Add the onion and cook, stirring occasionally, for 5 minutes, or until softened. Add the garlic, bell peppers, and eggplant and cook, stirring occasionally, for 5 minutes.

2 Add the rice and stir for about 1 minute, or until the grains are coated in oil. Add the Stock, tomatoes, saffron, and soaking water and season to taste with salt and pepper. Bring to a boil, reduce the heat, and simmer, shaking the skillet frequently and stirring occasionally, for 15 minutes.

3 Stir in the mushrooms, green beans, and pinto beans with their can juices. Cook for an additional 10 minutes, then serve.

caribbean rice & peas

cook: 1 hr 30 mins **prep: 10 mins** **serves 4**

Depending on whether you are on an eastern or western Caribbean island, this dish is known as "rice and peas" or "peas and rice." Either way, it is filling and delicious. It is suitable for vegetarians and vegans.

NUTRITIONAL INFORMATION

Calories	.349
Protein	.11g
Carbohydrate	.67g
Sugars	.5g
Fat	.6g
Saturates	.4g

INGREDIENTS

4 oz/115 g dried gunga peas, soaked overnight in enough water to cover

generous 1 cup long-grain rice

generous 2¾ cups water

2 oz/55 g creamed coconut

1 onion, chopped

2 garlic cloves, finely chopped

1 small red bell pepper, seeded and chopped

1 tbsp fresh thyme leaves

1 bay leaf

½ tsp ground allspice

salt and pepper

cook's tip

Gunga peas go by a variety of names, including pigeon, Congo, and Jamaica peas. Fresh gunga peas, sometimes known as Cajun peas, also feature in Caribbean cooking.

1 Drain the gunga peas and put them into a large pan. Add enough cold water to cover them by about 1 inch/2.5 cm. Bring to a boil and simmer for 1 hour, or until tender. Drain and return to the pan.

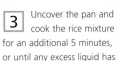

2 Add the rice, water, coconut, onion, garlic, bell pepper, thyme, bay leaf, and allspice and season to taste with salt and pepper. Bring to a boil, stirring constantly, until the creamed coconut has melted, then reduce the heat and simmer for 20 minutes.

3 Uncover the pan and cook the rice mixture for an additional 5 minutes, or until any excess liquid has evaporated. Fork through the rice to fluff up the grains, then serve.

kidney bean risotto

serves 4   **prep: 20 mins**   **cook: 1 hr**

The combination of nutty brown rice and kidney beans in this dish provides a perfect nutritional balance, as well as tasting wonderful. This dish is suitable for both vegetarians and vegans.

INGREDIENTS

4 tbsp olive oil

1 onion, chopped

2 garlic cloves, finely chopped

scant 1 cup brown rice

2½ cups Vegetable Stock (see page 13)

salt and pepper

1 red bell pepper, seeded and chopped

2 celery stalks, sliced

8 oz/225 g cremini mushrooms, thinly sliced

15 oz/425 g canned red kidney beans, drained and rinsed

3 tbsp chopped fresh parsley, plus extra to garnish

⅓ cup cashew nuts

NUTRITIONAL INFORMATION

Calories 456

Protein 14g

Carbohydrate 61g

Sugars 8g

Fat 20g

Saturates 2g

variation

You could also make this dish with a mixture of long-grain rice and wild rice instead of the brown rice. Follow the package instructions for cooking.

cook's tip

When cooking rice in a pan, make sure that the pan lid is tight-fitting, and resist the temptation to lift the lid during cooking.

1 Heat half the oil in a large, heavy-bottomed pan. Add the onion and cook, stirring occasionally, for 5 minutes, or until softened. Add half the garlic and cook, stirring frequently, for 2 minutes, then add the rice and stir for 1 minute, or until the grains are thoroughly coated with the oil. Add the Stock and a pinch of salt and bring to a boil, stirring constantly. Reduce the heat, cover, and simmer for 35–40 minutes, or until all the liquid has been absorbed.

2 Meanwhile, heat the remaining oil in a heavy-bottomed skillet. Add the bell pepper and celery and cook, stirring frequently, for 5 minutes. Add the sliced mushrooms and the remaining garlic and cook, stirring frequently, for 4–5 minutes.

3 Stir the rice into the skillet. Add the beans, parsley, and cashew nuts. Season to taste and cook, stirring constantly, until piping hot. Transfer to a warmed serving dish, sprinkle with extra parsley, and serve.

chow mein

serves 4   **prep: 15 mins**   **cook: 10 mins**

Egg noodles are cooked and then fried with a colorful variety of vegetables to make this well-known and ever-popular dish.

INGREDIENTS

1 lb 2 oz/500 g egg noodles

4 tbsp vegetable oil

1 onion, thinly sliced

2 carrots, cut into batons

4½ oz/125 g white mushrooms, quartered

4½ oz/125 g snow peas

½ cucumber, cut into batons

4½ oz/125 g fresh spinach, shredded

1¼ cups bean sprouts

2 tbsp dark soy sauce

1 tbsp sherry

1 tsp salt

1 tsp sugar

1 tsp cornstarch

1 tsp sesame oil

NUTRITIONAL INFORMATION

Calories 669

Protein 19g

Carbohydrate 100g

Sugars 9g

Fat 23g

Saturates 4g

variation

For a spicy hot chow mein, add 1 tablespoon chili sauce or substitute chili oil for the sesame oil.

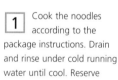

1 Cook the noodles according to the package instructions. Drain and rinse under cold running water until cool. Reserve until required.

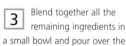

2 Heat 3 tablespoons of the vegetable oil in a preheated wok or skillet. Add the onion and carrots and stir-fry for 1 minute. Add the mushrooms, snow peas, and cucumber and stir-fry for 1 minute. Stir in the remaining vegetable oil and add the drained noodles, together with the spinach and bean sprouts.

3 Blend together all the remaining ingredients in a small bowl and pour over the noodles and vegetables. Stir-fry until the mixture is thoroughly heated through, transfer to a large, warmed serving dish, and serve immediately.

stir-fried japanese noodles

cook: 15 mins   **prep: 15 mins, plus 10 mins soaking**   **serves 4**

This quick dish is an ideal lunchtime meal, packed with whatever mixture of mushrooms you like in a sweet sauce.

NUTRITIONAL INFORMATION

Calories 379

Protein 12g

Carbohydrate 53g

Sugars 8g

Fat 13g

Saturates 3g

INGREDIENTS

8 oz/225 g Japanese egg noodles

2 tbsp corn oil

1 red onion, sliced

1 garlic clove, crushed

1 lb 2 oz/500 g mixed mushrooms, such as shiitake, oyster, and brown cap

12 oz/350 g bok choy

2 tbsp sweet sherry

6 tbsp soy sauce

4 scallions, sliced

1 tbsp sesame seeds, toasted

cook's tip

The variety of mushrooms in major food stores has greatly improved and a good mixture should be easily obtainable. If not, use the more common white and flat mushrooms.

1 Place the noodles in a large bowl, pour over enough boiling water to cover, and let soak for 10 minutes. Heat the oil in a large, preheated wok.

2 Add the red onion and garlic to the wok and stir-fry for 2–3 minutes, or until softened. Add the mushrooms to the wok and stir-fry for 5 minutes, or until softened. Drain the noodles and add to the wok.

3 Add the bok choy, sweet sherry, and soy sauce to the wok and toss to mix thoroughly. Stir-fry for 2–3 minutes, or until the liquid is just bubbling. Transfer the noodle mixture to warmed serving bowls, sprinkle with sliced scallions and toasted sesame seeds, and serve immediately.

side dishes

Vegetable accompaniments—whether served with a vegetarian main dish or
with meat, poultry, or fish—should never be afterthoughts, and their flavors, colors,
and textures should complement and enhance the main dish. This chapter offers
a wealth of choice to ensure a perfect match.

Potatoes may be a staple, but they don't have to be plain boiled or roasted
when you could serve Garlic Mash (see page 157) or Swiss Rösti (see page 162) instead. Popular
everyday vegetables are given a new treatment. Try Peas with Pearl Onions (see page 176) or
Cauliflower Fritters (see page 194), for example. Experiment with some new ideas or unusual
vegetables, such as Masala Okra (see page 178) or Orange & White Coulis (see page 184).

Salads are delicious accompaniments all year round, adding a crisp fresh touch
to any meal, and are usually quite quick and easy to prepare. This chapter concludes with a
selection of truly tasty fresh salads, made with a wide of variety of ingredients. You can make
great salads with almost any vegetable—it doesn't have to be lettuce. Try Roast Vegetable
Salad (see page 206) with a Mediterranean main course, Yam Salad (see page 202) with
a Caribbean dish, classic Caesar Salad (see page 210) with almost anything, and
Fruity Coleslaw (see page 200) for a taste revelation.

garlic mash

cook: 30 mins **prep: 15 mins** **serves 4**

variation

For a richer dish, substitute single cream for the milk and 8 tablespoons extra virgin olive oil for the butter.

Garlic adds an extra dimension to mashed potatoes—making a delicious change from a plain mash. Serve this flavorsome dish alongside Stuffed Bell Peppers with Cheese (see page 105) or Stuffed Onions (see page 104), or with hearty casseroles and stews.

INGREDIENTS

2 lb/900 g floury potatoes, cut into chunks

salt and pepper

8 garlic cloves, crushed

⅔ cup milk

6 tbsp butter

pinch of freshly grated nutmeg

cook's tip

To make mashed potatoes taste extra creamy and smooth, after mashing, use a hand-held whisk to beat the mixture thoroughly.

1 Put the potatoes into a large pan. Add enough water to cover and a pinch of salt. Bring to a boil and cook for 10 minutes. Add the garlic and cook for an additional 10–15 minutes, or until the potatoes are tender.

2 Drain the potatoes and garlic, reserving 3 tablespoons of the cooking liquid. Return the reserved cooking liquid to the pan, then add the milk and bring to simmering point. Add the butter, return the potatoes and garlic to the pan, and turn off the heat. Mash thoroughly with a potato masher.

3 Season the potato mixture to taste with nutmeg, salt, and pepper and beat thoroughly with a wooden spoon until light and fluffy. Serve immediately.

dauphinois potatoes

serves 4 **prep: 20 mins** **cook: 1 hr–1 hr 30 mins**

Cooking the humble potato in this classic way elevates it to gourmet heights. This delicious, creamy dish makes an excellent accompaniment for a vegetable bake—they can be cooked in the oven at the same time and served together.

INGREDIENTS

2 tbsp butter, diced, plus
extra for greasing

2 lb/900 g waxy potatoes,
peeled and very thinly sliced

1 large onion, finely chopped

generous 2 cups grated Swiss cheese

salt and pepper

⅔ cup light cream

NUTRITIONAL INFORMATION	
Calories	.530
Protein	.23g
Carbohydrate	.45g
Sugars	.6g
Fat	.30g
Saturates	.19g

variation

For Anna Potatoes, pour 1 cup of melted butter between 2 lb/900 g of seasoned, layered potato slices. Bake at 425°F/220°C for 1 hour.

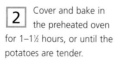

cook's tip

Waxy potatoes are usually recommended for dishes like this one because they are firmer than floury potatoes, and do not break up during the cooking process.

1 Preheat the oven to 375°F/190°C. Grease an ovenproof casserole with butter. Make a layer of potato slices in the bottom, dot with a little butter, sprinkle with onion and cheese, and season with salt and pepper. Pour in 2 tablespoons of the cream.

Continue making layers in this way, ending with a layer of cheese. Pour over any remaining cream.

2 Cover and bake in the preheated oven for 1–1½ hours, or until the potatoes are tender.

3 Remove the lid and place the casserole under a preheated hot broiler for 5 minutes, or until the top of the bake is golden brown and bubbling. Serve.

potato fans

⏲ **cook: 1 hr 15 mins**   ⏱ **prep: 10 mins**   **serves 4**

variation

Substitute parsley for the dill in
the dressing, or match the herb to
one used in the main dish that the
potatoes accompany.

*Potato fans look spectacular, and are the perfect accompaniment
to a dinner party dish. Here, they are served with a mayonnaise and
sour cream dressing, but this is optional. Without it, the dish is
suitable for vegans as well as vegetarians.*

INGREDIENTS

4 large baking potatoes	DRESSING (OPTIONAL)
3 garlic cloves,	4 tbsp Mayonnaise (see page 13)
very thinly sliced	4 tbsp sour cream
fresh dill sprigs, to garnish	4 tbsp chopped fresh dill

cook's tip

If you like crispy potato skins,
after slicing the potatoes, hold
each one together and rub the
skin lightly with olive oil before
inserting the garlic.

1 Preheat the oven
to 400°F/200°C. Make
a series of cuts in the potatoes
with a sharp knife, almost
cutting them through, so
they are sliced into thin fans.
Place garlic slices between
some of the potato slices.
Place the potatoes in an

ovenproof dish and bake in the
preheated oven for 1¼ hours,
until tender.

2 Meanwhile, make
the dressing. Mix the
ingredients together in a bowl,
cover with plastic wrap, and
reserve until required.

3 Transfer the potatoes
to a warmed serving
dish and serve immediately.
Hand the dressing separately
(if using) and garnish with
fresh dill sprigs.

rösti

serves 4   **prep: 15 mins, plus 1 hr** ⏱ **cooling/chilling**   **cook: 30 mins** ⏱

This popular Swiss side dish is a patty made with grated potatoes, and always proves to be a great favorite with children. It is suitable for both vegetarians and vegans.

INGREDIENTS

2 lb/900 g potatoes, unpeeled

2–4 tbsp unsalted butter or vegan margarine

1–2 tbsp olive oil

salt and pepper

NUTRITIONAL INFORMATION

Calories	264
Protein	. . . . .5g
Carbohydrate	. . . . .39g
Sugars	. . . . .1g
Fat	. . . . .11g
Saturates	. . . . .4g

cook's tip

Chilling the parboiled potatoes in the refrigerator at the end of Step 1 is not essential, but it will make them easier to handle when you grate them in Step 2.

1 Cook the potatoes in a pan of boiling water for 10 minutes. Drain and let cool completely. Chill in the refrigerator for at least 30 minutes.

2 Peel and coarsely grate the potatoes. Melt 2 tablespoons of the butter with 1 tablespoon of the oil in a heavy-bottomed 9-inch/23-cm skillet over medium heat. Spread out the grated potato evenly in the skillet, reduce the heat, and cook for 10 minutes.

3 Cover the skillet with a large plate, hold them together, and carefully invert. Slide the potato back into the skillet to cook the second side. Cook for an additional 10 minutes, adding more butter and oil, if necessary. Season to taste with salt and pepper and serve immediately.

refried beans

cook: 20 mins   **prep: 15 mins**   **serves 6**

Shortening is the traditional fat used for cooking this Mexican speciality, but vegetarians or anyone who is concerned about their cholesterol levels can use corn oil instead.

NUTRITIONAL INFORMATION

Calories	.338
Protein	.14g
Carbohydrate	.33g
Sugars	.7g
Fat	.18g
Saturates	.2g

INGREDIENTS

6–8 tbsp corn oil or shortening

1 onion, finely chopped

1 quantity of Frijoles

(see page 35)

fried tortillas, to serve

1 Heat 2 tablespoons of the corn oil in a large, heavy-bottomed skillet. Add the chopped onion and cook, stirring occasionally, for 5 minutes, or until softened. Add one fourth of the Frijoles.

2 Mash the Frijoles with a potato masher until well broken up. Add more Frijoles and more oil and mash again. Continue adding Frijoles and oil until all the beans have been incorporated and have formed a solid paste.

3 Cut the tortillas into fourths. Transfer the refried beans on to a warmed serving dish, shaping the paste into one large roll, and serve immediately, surrounded with the tortillas.

cook's tip

It is best not to use a skillet with a soft, nonstick coating for this dish, as mashing the beans inside the pan in Step 2 may damage its surface.

green herb rice

serves 4   **prep: 10 mins, plus 1 hr soaking**   **cook: 35 mins**

This is a deliciously different way to serve plain or fragrant rice for a special occasion, or simply to liven up a basic meal. The coconut milk adds richness, and the fresh herbs and chiles lend an extra mouthwatering kick to the flavor.

INGREDIENTS

2 tbsp olive oil

2½ cups basmati or Thai jasmine rice, soaked for 1 hour, washed and drained

generous 2¾ cups unsweetened coconut milk

1 tsp salt

1 bay leaf

2 tbsp chopped fresh cilantro

2 tbsp chopped fresh mint

2 fresh green chiles, seeded and finely chopped

lime wedges, to serve

NUTRITIONAL INFORMATION

Calories 652

Protein 15g

Carbohydrate 116g

Sugars 9g

Fat 17g

Saturates 6g

---

variation

Replace the lime wedges with lemon, if you like. The juice can also be squeezed over the rice.

cook's tip

When you are cooking the rice for this dish, keep the heat very low, otherwise it may stick to the bottom of the pan and burn.

1 Heat the olive oil in a large, heavy-bottomed pan over medium heat, add the rice, and stir until translucent. Add the coconut milk, salt, and bay leaf. Bring to a boil and cook until all the liquid is absorbed.

2 Reduce the heat to very low, cover the pan tightly and cook for 10 minutes, then remove the bay leaf and stir in the fresh cilantro, mint, and chiles.

3 Fork through the rice gently to fluff up the grains, then transfer to a warmed serving dish. Serve with lime wedges.

pulao rice

serves 4   **prep: 5 mins** ⟲   **cook: 25 mins** ⏲

Plain boiled rice is eaten by most people in India every day, but when guests are being entertained, spices such as cloves and cardamoms are added to the dish for a little extra interest.

INGREDIENTS

1 cup basmati rice

2 tbsp ghee or vegetable oil

3 green cardamoms

2 cloves

3 peppercorns

½ tsp salt

½ tsp saffron

1¾ cups water

NUTRITIONAL INFORMATION

Calories 265

Protein 4g

Carbohydrate 43g

Sugars 0g

Fat 10g

Saturates 6g

cook's tip

Saffron, the most expensive of all spices, comes from the stamens of a type of crocus. It gives dishes a rich, golden color and a slightly bitter taste. Saffron is sold as a powder or in strands.

1 Rinse the rice twice under cold running water and reserve.

2 Heat the ghee in a large, heavy-bottomed pan. Add the cardamoms, cloves, and peppercorns and cook, stirring constantly, for 1 minute.

3 Add the rice and stir-fry over medium heat for an additional 2 minutes.

4 Add the salt, saffron, and water to the rice mixture and reduce the heat. Cover the pan and simmer over low heat until the liquid has been absorbed.

5 Transfer the rice to a warmed serving dish and serve immediately.

chili roast potatoes

⏱ **cook: 35–40 mins**   ⏱ **prep: 10 mins**   **serves 4**

For this delicious side dish, small new potatoes are scrubbed and boiled in their skins, before being coated in a hot chili mixture and roasted to perfection in the oven.

NUTRITIONAL INFORMATION	
Calories	178
Protein	. . . . .2g
Carbohydrate	. . . . .18g
Sugars	. . . . .2g
Fat	. . . . .11g
Saturates	. . . . .1g

INGREDIENTS

1 lb 2 oz/500 g small new
potatoes, scrubbed

⅔ cup vegetable oil

1 tsp chili powder

½ tsp caraway seeds

1 tsp salt

1 tbsp chopped fresh basil

variation

To vary the flavor of this dish, use any other spice of your choice, such as curry powder or paprika.

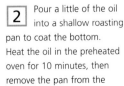

1 Preheat the oven to 400°F/200°C. Cook the new potatoes in a large pan of boiling water for 10 minutes, then drain thoroughly.

2 Pour a little of the oil into a shallow roasting pan to coat the bottom. Heat the oil in the preheated oven for 10 minutes, then remove the pan from the oven. Add the potatoes and brush them with the hot oil.

3 Mix the chili powder, caraway seeds, and salt together in a small bowl, then sprinkle the mixture evenly over the potatoes, turning them to coat. Add the remaining vegetable oil to the pan and return to the oven to roast for 15 minutes, or until the potatoes are cooked through.

4 Using a perforated spoon, remove the potatoes from the pan, draining well, and transfer to a large, warmed serving dish. Sprinkle chopped basil over the top and serve immediately.

fennel with tomatoes & olives

cook: 25 mins　　　　**prep: 10 mins**　　　　**serves 6**

Full of Italian flavors, this side dish is an excellent choice for a dinner party, and would go well with both vegetarian and fish dishes. The unique flavor of the black olives perfectly complements the tomatoes and the slightly aniseed taste of the fennel. The dish is suitable for both vegetarians and vegans.

INGREDIENTS

2 fennel bulbs

1 tbsp olive oil

1 onion, thinly sliced

2 tomatoes, peeled and chopped

2 oz/55 g black olives, pitted

2 tbsp torn fresh basil leaves

pepper

variation

For a slightly richer side dish, vegetarians and meat-eaters could stir in 2 tablespoons of light cream just before serving in Step 3.

cook's tip

Do not slice the fennel too far in advance, as the cut surfaces discolor on exposure to air. Alternatively, put the slices in a bowl of water acidulated with 2 tablespoons of lemon juice, and drain before using.

1 Cut off the fennel fronds and chop them. Cut the fennel bulbs in half lengthwise, then slice thinly.

2 Heat the oil in a heavy-bottomed skillet. Add the onion and cook over low heat, stirring occasionally, for 5 minutes, or until softened. Add the fennel slices and cook, stirring occasionally, for an additional 10 minutes.

3 Increase the heat and add the tomatoes and olives. Cook, stirring frequently, for 10 minutes, then stir in the basil and season to taste with pepper. Transfer to a warmed serving dish, garnish with the fennel fronds, and serve.

charbroiled vegetables with salsa verde

serves 6   **prep: 20 mins, plus** ⟳   **cook: 13–15 mins** ⏲
40 mins cooling/chilling

You can cook this colorful collection of vegetables under the broiler or on a barbecue grill. They are the perfect accompaniment for crêpes or burgers. This dish is suitable for vegetarians and vegans.

INGREDIENTS

2 yams (dark sweet potatoes), sliced

3 zucchini, halved lengthwise

salt

3 red bell peppers, seeded and
cut into fourths

olive oil, for brushing

SALSA VERDE

2 fresh green chiles, halved
and seeded

8 scallions, coarsely chopped

2 garlic cloves, coarsely chopped

1 tbsp capers

1 bunch of fresh parsley,
coarsely chopped

grated rind and juice of 1 lime

4 tbsp lemon juice

6 tbsp olive oil

1 tbsp green Tabasco sauce

pepper

NUTRITIONAL INFORMATION

Calories	.172
Protein	.2g
Carbohydrate	.15g
Sugars	.6g
Fat	.12g
Saturates	.2g

variation

Substitute 2 thickly sliced eggplants for the yams for a slightly more Mediterranean dish. Salt the eggplants with the zucchini.

cook's tip

If using capers bottled in vinegar, rinse them before using. If using salted capers, simply brush them with your fingertips to remove some of the salt.

1 Cook the yam slices in boiling water for 5 minutes. Drain and let cool. Sprinkle the cut sides of the zucchini with salt and let stand for 30 minutes.

2 Meanwhile, make the salsa verde. Put the chiles, scallions, and garlic into a food processor and process briefly. Add the capers and parsley and pulse until finely chopped. Scrape the mixture into a serving bowl and stir in the lime rind and juice, lemon juice, olive oil, and Tabasco. Season with pepper, cover with plastic wrap, and chill in the refrigerator until required.

3 Rinse the salted zucchini and pat dry with paper towels. Brush the yam slices, zucchini, and bell peppers with olive oil and spread out on a broiler rack. Cook under a preheated hot broiler or lit barbecue grill, turning once and brushing with more oil, for 8–10 minutes, or until tender and lightly charred. Serve with the salsa verde.

braised red cabbage

cook: 5 mins **prep: 15 mins** **serves 6**

NUTRITIONAL INFORMATION

Calories 170

Protein 3g

Carbohydrate 29g

Sugars 25g

Fat 4g

Saturates 0g

variation

Add 1 teaspoon of grated fresh gingerroot with the cloves in Step 2 for a slightly hotter flavor.

A delicious sharp-sweet taste and an eye-catching color make this braised red cabbage a vegetable accompaniment with attitude, sure to attract attention at a dinner party. The apples give the dish a tangy sweetness and a mix of interesting textures. It is suitable for both vegetarians and vegans.

INGREDIENTS

2 tbsp corn oil

2 onions, thinly sliced

2 eating apples, peeled, cored and thinly sliced

2 lb/900 g red cabbage, cored and shredded

4 tbsp red wine vinegar

2 tbsp sugar

¼ tsp ground cloves

⅓ cup raisins

½ cup red wine

salt and pepper

2 tbsp redcurrant jelly

cook's tip

This dish does not have to be cooked on the stove—you can also braise the cabbage in a preheated oven, 350°F/180°C, for 1 hour.

1 Heat the oil in a large pan. Add the onions and cook, stirring occasionally, for 10 minutes, or until softened and golden. Stir in the apple slices and cook for 3 minutes.

2 Add the cabbage, vinegar, sugar, cloves, raisins, and red wine and season to taste. Bring to a boil, stirring occasionally. Reduce the heat, cover, and cook, stirring occasionally, for 40 minutes, or until the cabbage is tender and most of the liquid has been absorbed.

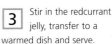

3 Stir in the redcurrant jelly, transfer to a warmed dish and serve.

candied sweet potatoes

serves 6   **prep: 15 mins** ⏲   **cook: 25 mins** ⏲

A taste of the Caribbean is introduced in this recipe, where sweet potatoes are cooked with sugar, fresh lime juice, and a dash of brandy. This dish makes the perfect accompaniment to numerous main meals, both vegetarian and fish dishes. To make it suitable for vegans, substitute the butter for vegan margarine.

INGREDIENTS

1 lb 8 oz/675 g sweet potatoes, sliced

3 tbsp butter

1 tbsp lime juice

scant ⅓ cup soft dark brown sugar

1 tbsp brandy

grated rind of 1 lime

lime wedges, to garnish

variation

Replace the lime with lemon and substitute the brandy with the same amount of rum, if you prefer.

cook's tip

Sweet potatoes have a pinkish skin and either white, yellow, or orange flesh (dark fleshed sweet potatoes are often known as yams). It doesn't matter which type is used for this dish.

1 Cook the sweet potatoes in a large, heavy-bottomed pan of boiling water for 5 minutes, or until softened. To test if the potatoes are soft, prick with a fork. Remove the sweet potatoes with a perforated spoon and drain thoroughly.

2 Melt the butter in a large skillet. Add the lime juice and sugar and heat gently, stirring, to dissolve the sugar.

3 Stir the sweet potatoes and the brandy into the sugar and lime juice mixture. Cook over low heat for 10 minutes, or until the potato slices are cooked through.

4 Sprinkle the lime rind over the top of the sweet potatoes and mix well.

5 Transfer the candied sweet potatoes to a large, warmed serving plate. Garnish with lime wedges and serve immediately.

peas with pearl onions

This is a delightful dish when made with the first fresh peas of the season, and its subtle, creamy flavor goes well with a wide variety of vegetarian and meat-based main meals.

INGREDIENTS

1 tbsp unsalted butter

6 oz/175 g pearl onions

2 lb/900 g fresh peas, shelled

½ cup water

2 tbsp all-purpose flour

⅔ cup heavy cream

1 tbsp chopped fresh parsley

salt and pepper

1 tbsp lemon juice

NUTRITIONAL INFORMATION

Calories 317

Protein 8g

Carbohydrate 22g

Sugars 6g

Fat 23g

Saturates 14g

variation

To make a slightly more substantial dish, substitute 4 lb 8 oz/2 kg of young fava beans for the peas in Step 1.

1 Melt the butter in a large, heavy-bottomed pan. Add the whole pearl onions and cook, stirring occasionally, for 5 minutes. Add the fresh peas and cook, stirring constantly, for 3 minutes, then add the water and bring to a boil. Reduce the heat, partially cover, and simmer for 10 minutes.

2 Beat the flour into the cream. Remove the pan from the heat and stir in the cream and parsley. Season.

3 Return the pan to the heat and cook, stirring, for 3 minutes, or until thickened. Stir in the lemon juice and serve.

green beans with tomatoes

⏱ **cook: 35 mins**   ⏲ **prep: 10 mins**   **serves 4**

The rich tomato sauce gives extra flavor to these succulent green beans. You can serve this side dish hot or cold. It is suitable for both vegetarians and vegans.

NUTRITIONAL INFORMATION	
Calories	130
Protein	3g
Carbohydrate	9g
Sugars	7g
Fat	9g
Saturates	1g

INGREDIENTS

3 tbsp olive oil

1 red onion, thinly sliced

12 oz/350 g tomatoes, peeled and chopped

½ cup water

8 fresh basil leaves, torn

salt and pepper

1 lb/450 g green beans

cook's tip

There are lots of varieties of green beans—wax, cannellini, yard-long, and even purple "green" beans. All of these varieties are suitable for this recipe.

1 Heat the oil in a large, heavy-bottomed skillet over low heat. Add the onion and cook, stirring occasionally, for 5 minutes, or until softened.

2 Add the chopped tomatoes and cook, stirring occasionally, for 7–8 minutes, or until softened. Add the water and basil and season to taste.

3 Add the beans and turn to coat in the sauce. Cover and cook, stirring occasionally, for 20 minutes, or until tender, adding a little more water if necessary.

Transfer to a warmed serving dish and serve immediately. Alternatively, transfer to a dish and let cool to room temperature before serving.

masala okra

serves 4   **prep: 10 mins**   **cook: 15 mins**

Also known as bhindi, gumbo, and ladies' fingers, okra are small, five-sided, tapering pods that are very popular in the cuisines of the south, and in India and the Caribbean. This is a spicy Indian dish that would go well with any type of curry. It is suitable for both vegetarians and vegans.

INGREDIENTS

1 tbsp ground coriander	2 tbsp chopped fresh cilantro
1 tbsp ground cumin	pinch of salt
1 tsp chili powder	3 tbsp peanut oil
½ tsp ground turmeric	½ tsp black mustard seeds
1 tbsp dry unsweetened coconut	½ tsp cumin seeds
pinch of sugar	1 lb/450 g okra
1 tbsp lime juice	chopped tomato, to garnish

NUTRITIONAL INFORMATION

Calories 134

Protein 4g

Carbohydrate 5g

Sugars 4g

Fat 11g

Saturates 3g

variation

If you can't find any peanut oil, substitute corn oil, which will work just as well for this dish.

cook's tip

Preparing okra for cooking is very simple. Wash it in cold water and pat dry with paper towels, then trim the ends with a sharp knife, if you like.

1 Mix the ground coriander, ground cumin, chili powder, turmeric, coconut, sugar, lime juice, cilantro, and salt together in a bowl.

2 Heat the oil in a preheated wok or heavy-bottomed skillet. Add the mustard seeds and cumin seeds and cook, stirring constantly, for 2 minutes, or until the seeds begin to release their aroma and pop. Stir in the coconut mixture and cook, stirring, for 2 minutes.

3 Add the okra to the wok and stir to mix with the spices. Cover and cook for 10 minutes, or until tender. Transfer to a warmed serving dish, garnish with chopped tomato, and serve.

baked celery with cream

cook: 40 mins　　　**prep: 15 mins**　　　**serves 4**

variation

Substitute coarsely chopped walnuts for the pecan halves to give the dish a stronger flavor.

This dish is sprinkled with a layer of bread crumbs and Parmesan cheese to make a crunchy topping, underneath which is hidden a mixture of celery and pecans, drenched in a generous helping of light cream. Dried spices and a little crushed garlic give this tasty accompaniment an extra depth of flavor.

INGREDIENTS

1 head of celery	⅔ cup light cream
½ tsp ground cumin	salt and pepper
½ tsp ground coriander	1 cup fresh whole-wheat
1 garlic clove, crushed	bread crumbs
1 red onion, thinly sliced	¼ cup freshly grated
scant ½ cup pecan halves	Parmesan cheese
⅔ cup Vegetable Stock	celery leaves, to garnish
(see page 13)	

cook's tip

Once grated, Parmesan cheese quickly loses its "bite," so it is best to grate only the amount you need for the recipe. Wrap the rest tightly in foil and it will keep for several months in the refrigerator.

1 Preheat the oven to 400°F/200°C. Trim the celery and cut into short, thin sticks. Place the celery in an ovenproof dish with the ground cumin and coriander, garlic, red onion, and pecans.

2 Mix the Stock and cream together in a pitcher and pour over the vegetables. Season to taste with salt and pepper. Mix the bread crumbs and cheese together in a small bowl and sprinkle over the top to cover the vegetables.

3 Cook in the preheated oven for 40 minutes, or until the vegetables are tender and the top is crispy. Garnish with celery leaves and serve.

indonesian deep-fried onions

serves 6   **prep: 10 mins,** ↺ **plus 2 hrs drying**   **cook: 20 mins** ⏱

This is Indonesia's most popular garnish, but it also makes a tasty accompaniment to many Western-style main dishes. It is suitable for both vegetarians and vegans.

INGREDIENTS

1 lb/450 g small onions

peanut or corn oil,
for deep-frying

NUTRITIONAL INFORMATION	
Calories 76	
Protein 1g	
Carbohydrate 6g	
Sugars 4g	
Fat 6g	
Saturates 1g	

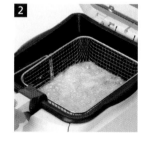

cook's tip

It is important that the onions are well dried before cooking, or they will not become crisp. Small onions tend to be less watery than large ones.

1 Using a sharp knife, slice the onions as thinly and evenly as possible. Spread out the slices on paper towels in a well-ventilated place and let stand for up to 2 hours to dry out.

2 Heat the oil in a preheated wok or deep-fryer to 350–375°F/180–190°C, or until a cube of bread browns in 30 seconds. Add the onions, in batches, and cook until crisp and golden. Remove the onions with a perforated spoon and drain on paper towels. Transfer to a large serving dish and serve.

braised belgian endive

cook: 50 mins   **prep: 15 mins**   **serves 6**

The Belgian endive is a much underrated vegetable, yet it can be made into a very attractive side dish, and provides a refreshing, slightly bitter contrast to a rich main meal.

NUTRITIONAL INFORMATION

Calories	.40
Protein	.1g
Carbohydrate	.4g
Sugars	.2g
Fat	.3g
Saturates	.2g

INGREDIENTS

generous 2 cups Vegetable Stock (see page 13)

1 bay leaf

6 fresh parsley sprigs

2 fresh thyme sprigs

12 heads of Belgian endive

4 tbsp lemon juice

6 tbsp fresh parsley leaves

5 tbsp light cream

salt and pepper

variation

This dish also works well with radicchio, which is closely related to endives. Unfortunately, radicchio doesn't retain its vibrant red color when cooked.

1 Pour the Stock into a large, heavy-bottomed pan and bring to a boil. Tie the bay leaf, parsley, and thyme together, add to the pan, cover, and simmer for 10 minutes.

2 Add the endive and lemon juice, cover, and simmer for 20–25 minutes, or until the endive is tender.

3 Remove the endive with a perforated spoon, reserving the cooking liquid. Transfer to a warmed serving dish and keep warm. Remove and discard the herbs.

4 Return the cooking liquid to a boil and continue to boil, uncovered, for 15 minutes, or until reduced to ⅔ cup.

5 Meanwhile, blanch the parsley leaves in boiling water for 1 minute, then drain and place in a food processor. Process until very finely chopped. With the motor still running, gradually add the cooking liquid.

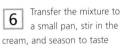

6 Transfer the mixture to a small pan, stir in the cream, and season to taste with salt and pepper. Heat through gently, but do not let it boil. Pour over the endive and serve immediately.

orange & white coulis

serves 4   **prep: 15 mins**   **cook: 10 mins**

Steaming is a healthy way to cook and is ideally suited to vegetables, as it helps to preserve the valuable vitamins and minerals which would otherwise leak out into the cooking water. This is an ingenious way to encourage fussy children to eat vegetables because it looks so pretty.

INGREDIENTS

ORANGE COULIS

⅔ cup freshly squeezed orange juice

8 oz/225 g carrots, thinly sliced, plus a few strips of carrot to garnish

2 oz/55 g ricotta cheese

pinch of ground coriander

1 tsp lemon juice

salt and white pepper

WHITE COULIS

⅔ cup Vegetable Stock (see page 13)

8 oz/225 g parsnips, thinly sliced

2 oz/55 g ricotta cheese

pinch of freshly grated nutmeg

1 tsp lemon juice

salt and white pepper

pinch of chopped fresh parsley, to garnish

NUTRITIONAL INFORMATION

Calories	99
Protein	3g
Carbohydrate	16g
Sugars	12g
Fat	3g
Saturates	1g

variation

Steam 8 oz/225 g cabbage over ⅔ cup of Vegetable Stock, process, and mix with ricotta cheese, fresh mint, and lemon juice.

cook's tip

Any colored vegetable can be used to make a coulis (see variation above). Follow the same proportions of vegetable, ricotta cheese, and lemon juice. Add 1 tablespoon of chopped herbs, if you like.

1 To make the orange coulis, pour the orange juice into a small pan and bring to a boil. Place the carrot slices in a steamer on top of the pan, cover tightly, and steam for 10 minutes. Meanwhile, to make the white coulis, place the Vegetable Stock in a small pan and bring to a boil. Place the parsnip slices in a steamer on top of the pan, cover tightly and steam for 10 minutes.

2 Transfer the carrots and orange juice for the orange coulis to a blender or food processor and process to a paste. Scrape into a bowl, then stir in the ricotta cheese, coriander, and lemon juice and season to taste. Keep warm.

3 Transfer the parsnips and Vegetable Stock for the white coulis to a blender or food processor and process to a paste. Scrape into a bowl, then stir in the ricotta cheese, nutmeg, and lemon juice and season to taste.

4 Spoon the coulis into serving dishes, and make decorative marks on the surface with a fork. Garnish the orange coulis with strips of carrot and the white coulis with a pinch of parsley and serve.

boston beans

These are the original baked beans and you will find them much tastier than the canned variety. They were traditionally cooked with salt pork, but this dish is suitable for vegetarians and vegans.

INGREDIENTS

1 lb 2 oz/500 g dried Great Northern
beans, soaked overnight in
enough cold water to cover
2 onions, chopped
2 large tomatoes, peeled and chopped
2 tsp mustard
2 tbsp molasses
salt and pepper

NUTRITIONAL INFORMATION

Calories	217
Protein	14g
Carbohydrate	40g
Sugars	9g
Fat	1g
Saturates	0g

variation

If you are a meat-eater and want to cook the original one-pot meal, add 12 oz/350 g diced salt pork to the casserole with the onions in Step 1.

1 Preheat the oven to 275°F/140°C. Drain the beans and place in a large pan. Add enough cold water to cover, bring to a boil, then reduce the heat and simmer for 15 minutes. Drain, reserving 1¼ cups of the cooking liquid. Transfer the beans to a large casserole and add the onions.

2 Return the reserved cooking liquid to the pan and add the tomatoes. Bring to a boil, then reduce the heat and simmer for 10 minutes. Remove from the heat, stir in the mustard and molasses, and season to taste with salt and pepper.

3 Pour the mixture into the casserole and bake in the preheated oven for 5 hours. Serve immediately.

steamed vegetable pockets

cook: 8–10 mins   **prep: 15 mins**   **serves 4**

Baby vegetables are cooked whole so that they lose none of their flavor, texture, or goodness. Serve them in their pockets for diners to unwrap at the table. This dish is suitable for vegetarians and vegans.

NUTRITIONAL INFORMATION

Calories 170

Protein 3g

Carbohydrate 11g

Sugars 10g

Fat 12g

Saturates 8g

INGREDIENTS

4 oz/115 g green beans

2 oz/55 g snow peas

12 baby carrots

8 pearl onions or shallots

12 baby turnips

8 radishes

salt and pepper

¼ cup unsalted butter or
vegetarian margarine

4 thinly pared strips of lemon rind

4 tsp finely chopped fresh chervil

4 tbsp dry white wine

variation

Substitute 4 tablespoons of olive oil for the butter or margarine, chopped fresh mint for the chervil, and cherry tomatoes for the radishes.

1 Cut out 4 double-thickness circles of waxed paper about 12 inches/ 30 cm in diameter.

2 Divide the green beans, snow peas, carrots, onions, turnips, and radishes between the circles, placing them on one half. Season with salt and pepper and dot with the butter. Divide the lemon rind between the pockets, then sprinkle with the chervil and drizzle with the wine. Fold over the double layer of paper, twisting the edges together to seal.

3 Bring a large pan of water to a boil and place a steamer on top. Put the pockets in the steamer, cover tightly, and steam for 8–10 minutes. Remove the pockets from the steamer and serve immediately.

sesame stir-fry

cook: 12 mins   **prep: 10 mins**   **serves 4**

NUTRITIONAL INFORMATION	
Calories 165	
Protein 6g	
Carbohydrate 6g	
Sugars 2g	
Fat 13g	
Saturates 2g	

Stir-fried vegetables are wonderfully quick and easy and can be served as part of a Chinese meal or with a Western main dish. This dish is suitable for vegetarians and vegans.

INGREDIENTS

3 tbsp peanut or corn oil

1 tbsp sesame oil

12 garlic cloves, finely chopped

8 oz/225 g broccoli, cut into florets

4 oz/115 g snow peas or sugar snap peas

1 head of Napa cabbage, shredded

6 scallions, chopped

2 tbsp dark soy sauce

2 tbsp Chinese rice wine

3 tbsp water

1 tbsp sesame seeds, toasted, to garnish

variation

Use only half a head of Napa cabbage and add 4 oz/115 g of thinly sliced carrots and 4 oz/115 g of baby corn cobs with the broccoli in Step 1.

cook's tip

A wok is preferable to a skillet for stir-fries because it has a larger heated surface area than a flat-bottomed pan. This allows the vegetables to cook more evenly.

1 Heat both oils in a preheated wok or large, heavy-bottomed skillet. Add the garlic and stir-fry for 30 seconds. Add the broccoli and stir-fry for 3 minutes. Add the snow peas and stir-fry for 2 minutes, then add the shredded Napa cabbage and scallions and stir-fry for an additional 2 minutes.

2 Stir in the soy sauce, Chinese rice wine, and water and cook, stirring constantly, for 3–4 minutes.

Transfer to a warmed serving dish, sprinkle with the toasted sesame seeds, and serve.

fava beans with summer savory

serves 4   **prep: 15 mins**   **cook: 20 mins**

This nutritious dish is high in soluble fiber, which helps to keep cholesterol levels down. It uses a traditional combination of ingredients—summer savory is often grown with fava beans, as it helps to protect them against black fly, so it is natural to cook them together, too. This dish is suitable for vegetarians and vegans.

INGREDIENTS

2 lb/900 g fava bean pods	¼ cup butter or
salt and pepper	vegetarian margarine
1 fresh summer savory sprig	1 tbsp lemon juice
	1 tbsp chopped fresh
	summer savory

NUTRITIONAL INFORMATION

Calories 180
Protein 8g
Carbohydrate 10g
Sugars 2g
Fat 13g
Saturates 8g

---

variation

Tenderly cooked fava beans also go well with other chopped fresh herbs, such as chives and parsley.

cook's tip

If using mature fava beans, skin them before tossing them in the melted butter. The best way to do this is to blanch the beans—the skins should then slip off easily.

1 Reserve 1 pod and shell the remaining beans. Bring a large pan of lightly salted water to a boil and add the beans, the reserved pod, and the sprig of summer savory. Cover and simmer for 10–15 minutes, or until the beans are tender.

2 Drain the beans and discard the pod and sprig of summer savory. Melt the butter in the pan over low heat, add the lemon juice and beans, and season to taste with pepper. Toss the beans to coat them in the butter.

3 Transfer the beans to a warmed serving dish. Sprinkle them with the chopped summer savory and serve immediately.

italian zucchini

cook: 20 mins   **prep: 10 mins**   **serves 4**

NUTRITIONAL INFORMATION	
Calories	100
Protein	3g
Carbohydrate	10g
Sugars	3g
Fat	6g
Saturates	1g

variation

You can substitute other fresh herbs of your choice for the marjoram and parsley to bring a slightly different flavor to this dish.

This quick and easy recipe is a very tasty way to cook zucchini—the onion, garlic, stock, and fresh herbs help to bring out the full flavor of these vegetables, and cooking them very gently in olive oil gives them a deliciously soft, buttery texture. This dish is suitable for both vegetarians and vegans.

INGREDIENTS

2 tbsp olive oil

1 large onion, chopped

1 garlic clove, finely chopped

5 zucchini, sliced

⅔ cup Vegetable Stock

(see page 13)

1 tsp chopped fresh marjoram

salt and pepper

1 tbsp chopped fresh flatleaf parsley, to garnish

cook's tip

Always leave the skin on zucchini, because this is where most of their nutrients are stored. They provide plenty of vitamin C and folic acid.

1   Heat the oil in a large, heavy-bottomed skillet. Add the chopped onion and garlic and cook, stirring occasionally, for 5 minutes, or until softened. Add the zucchini and cook, stirring

frequently, for 3–4 minutes, or until they are just beginning to brown.

2   Add the Stock and marjoram and season to taste with salt and pepper.

Simmer for 10 minutes, or until almost all of the liquid has evaporated. Transfer to a warmed serving dish, sprinkle with the parsley, and serve.

cauliflower fritters

serves 4 **prep: 15 mins** **cook: 15 mins**

These battered florets make an unusual accompaniment to vegetable bakes or gratins such as Cheese & Tomato Bake (see page 112) or Vegetarian Lasagna (see page 120). Alternatively, it could also be served as a dinner party appetizer, with a delicious dipping sauce, such as Garlic Mayonnaise (see page 40).

INGREDIENTS

1 large cauliflower,
cut into florets
generous ¾ cup all-purpose flour
pinch of salt
pinch of dried thyme

2 eggs, separated
⅔ cup water
4 tbsp milk
corn oil, for deep-frying

NUTRITIONAL INFORMATION	
Calories	.253
Protein	.10g
Carbohydrate	.26g
Sugars	.4g
Fat	.13g
Saturates	.2g

variation

You can cook other vegetables in the same way, without blanching. Try wedges of red bell pepper, eggplant or zucchini slices, or mushrooms.

cook's tip

The oil needs to be very hot to cook the batter successfully. The temperature will drop during the cooking process, so be sure to let the oil re-heat between batches.

1 Blanch the cauliflower in a large pan of boiling water for 5 minutes. Drain well and pat dry with paper towels.

2 Sift the flour and salt into a bowl and add the thyme, egg yolks, and water. Beat well with a wooden spoon until smooth.

Beat in the milk. Whisk the egg whites in a separate clean, grease-free bowl until stiff peaks form, then gently fold the egg whites into the batter.

3 Heat the oil in a deep-fryer to 350–375°F/180–190°C, or until a cube of bread browns in 30 seconds.

Dip the cauliflower florets in the batter to coat, then cook, in batches, until golden. Drain on paper towels and serve.

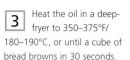

corn salad with beet & walnuts

serves 4   **prep: 10 mins**   **cook: 0 mins**

This simple, mouthwatering side salad has a delicate, subtle flavor that will not overpower the main meal. It will also add a splash of vibrant color to any dinner table.

INGREDIENTS

6 oz/175 g corn salad

4 small beets, cooked and diced

2 tbsp chopped walnuts

DRESSING

2 tbsp lemon juice

2 garlic cloves, finely chopped

1 tbsp Dijon mustard

pinch of sugar

salt and pepper

½ cup corn oil

½ cup sour cream

NUTRITIONAL INFORMATION

Calories 339

Protein 3g

Carbohydrate 7g

Sugars 7g

Fat 33g

Saturates 7g

cook's tip

You can prepare the dressing in advance, but do not pour it over the salad until you are ready to serve it, otherwise the leaves will become soggy.

1 To make the dressing, place the lemon juice, garlic, mustard, and sugar in a bowl, mix well, then season to taste with salt and pepper. Gradually whisk in the oil. Lightly beat the sour cream, then whisk it into the dressing.

2 Place the corn salad in a bowl and pour over one-third of the dressing. Toss to coat.

3 Divide the lettuce between 4 bowls. Top each portion with diced beet and drizzle over the remaining dressing. Sprinkle with chopped walnuts and serve.

spinach & garlic salad

cook: 15 mins   **prep: 5 mins**   **serves 4**

This robust salad goes especially well with pasta dishes. Roasting garlic gives it a deliciously sweet flavor. This dish is suitable for both vegetarians and vegans.

NUTRITIONAL INFORMATION

Calories 228

Protein 6g

Carbohydrate 3g

Sugars 2g

Fat 21g

Saturates 2g

INGREDIENTS

12 garlic cloves, unpeeled

4 tbsp olive oil

1 lb/450 g fresh baby spinach leaves

½ cup chopped walnuts or pine nuts

2 tbsp lemon juice

salt and pepper

1 Preheat the oven to 375°F/190°C. Place the garlic cloves in an ovenproof dish, add 2 tablespoons of the olive oil, and toss to coat thoroughly. Roast in the oven for 15 minutes.

2 Transfer the garlic and olive oil to a salad bowl. Add the spinach leaves, chopped walnuts, lemon juice, and remaining olive oil. Toss well to coat and season to taste with salt and pepper.

3 Transfer the salad to individual dishes and serve immediately, while the garlic is still warm. Diners squeeze the softened garlic out of the skins at the table.

variation

Substitute young sorrel leaves for the baby spinach leaves to give this salad a delicious, lemony flavor.

green vegetable salad

cook: 10 mins

prep: 10 mins, plus 15 mins cooling

serves 4

This salad uses lots of green-colored ingredients, which look and taste wonderful with the minty yogurt dressing. It is a highly nutritious side dish, packed with vitamin C and folic acid, and tastes great served with Vegetarian Lasagna (see page 120) or Spinach & Cheese Crêpes (see page 132).

variation

Sprinkle the finished dish with a few chopped walnuts to add even more crunch to this salad, if you like.

INGREDIENTS

2 zucchini, cut into batons

3½ oz/100 g green beans, cut into 3 pieces

salt and pepper

1 green bell pepper, seeded and cut into strips

2 celery stalks, sliced

1 bunch of watercress or corn salad

DRESSING

generous ¾ cup plain yogurt

1 garlic clove, crushed

2 tbsp chopped fresh mint

cook's tip

The salad must be served as soon as the yogurt dressing has been added—the dressing will begin to separate if kept for any length of time.

1 Cook the zucchini batons and green beans in a small pan of salted boiling water for 7–8 minutes, or until tender. Drain the vegetables, and let cool completely. Place the cooled zucchini and beans in a large serving bowl with the pepper, celery, and watercress and toss to mix.

2 To make the dressing, place the yogurt, garlic, and mint in a small bowl and mix thoroughly. Season to taste with pepper, then spoon the dressing on to the salad and serve immediately.

fruity coleslaw

Most ready-made coleslaw seems to be smothered in a strong vinegar dressing. You will notice the difference immediately when you taste this colorful, home-made version, made with raw cabbage, a wide selection of fruit, and a handful of crunchy pine nuts. This dish is suitable for vegetarians and vegans.

INGREDIENTS

½ small red cabbage, thinly shredded
½ small white cabbage, thinly shredded
6 oz/175 g dried dates, pitted and chopped
1 red eating apple
2 green eating apples
4 tbsp lemon juice
scant ¼ cup pine nuts, toasted

DRESSING

5 tbsp olive oil
2 tbsp cider vinegar
1 tsp clear honey
salt and pepper

NUTRITIONAL INFORMATION

Calories 234

Protein 3g

Carbohydrate 30g

Sugars 30g

Fat 12g

Saturates 2g

variation

Substitute coarsely chopped walnuts for the pine nuts, or raisins for the dates, if you prefer.

cook's tip

A good way to mix salad dressings is to put all the ingredients into a screw-top jar, put on the lid, and shake vigorously to combine.

1 Place the red and white cabbage in a salad bowl with the dates and toss well to mix.

2 Core the apples, but do not peel them. Thinly slice and place in a separate bowl. Add the lemon juice and toss well to coat to prevent discoloration. Add them to the salad bowl.

3 To make the dressing, whisk the oil, vinegar, and honey together in a small bowl and season to taste with salt and pepper. Pour the dressing over the salad and toss. Sprinkle with the pine nuts, toss lightly and serve.

yam salad

serves 4　　　　**prep: 10 mins** ⏲　　　　**cook: 15 mins** ⏲

This unusual salad, with its peppery dressing, is best eaten while it is still warm. It is full of protein and vitamins, and can be served on its own with some crusty bread as a satisfying light meal.

INGREDIENTS

1 yam (dark sweet potato), peeled and diced

2 carrots, sliced

3 tomatoes, seeded and chopped

3 oz/85 g canned chickpeas, drained

8 iceberg lettuce leaves

1 tbsp golden raisins

1 tbsp chopped walnuts

1 small onion, thinly sliced into rings

DRESSING

6 tbsp plain yogurt

1 tbsp clear honey

1 tsp coarsely ground pepper

salt

NUTRITIONAL INFORMATION

Calories	192
Protein	7g
Carbohydrate	33g
Sugars	23g
Fat	4g
Saturates	1g

cook's tip

If the salad greens slip down the sides of the bowl when you try to line it, hold on to them with one hand and spoon in some vegetable mixture to weigh them down.

1 Cook the yam in a large pan of boiling water for 10 minutes. Add the carrots and cook for an additional 3–5 minutes, or until the yam is tender, but still firm to the bite. Drain well and place in a large bowl. Add the chopped tomatoes and chickpeas to the yam and carrots and mix together thoroughly.

2 Line a salad bowl with the lettuce leaves and spoon the vegetable mixture into the center. Sprinkle with the golden raisins, walnuts, and onion rings.

3 To make the dressing, place the yogurt, honey, and pepper in a small serving bowl and whisk thoroughly with a fork. Season to taste with salt. Serve the yam salad warm and hand the dressing separately.

potato & apple salad

cook: 20 mins   **prep: 10 mins**   **serves 6**

Bite-size baby new potatoes are perfect for salads, as they look tempting and have a wonderful flavor and texture, which works especially well combined with creamy mayonnaise.

NUTRITIONAL INFORMATION

Calories 219

Protein 4g

Carbohydrate 29g

Sugars 6g

Fat 11g

Saturates 2g

INGREDIENTS

2 lb/900 g baby new
potatoes, unpeeled

2 green eating apples

4 scallions, chopped

4 celery stalks, chopped

⅔ cup Mayonnaise (see page 13)

salt and pepper

variation

For extra flavor, stir
1 tablespoon of snipped
fresh chives into the
Mayonnaise before adding
it to the salad in Step 3.

1 Cook the baby new potatoes in a large pan of lightly salted boiling water for 20 minutes, or until tender. Drain well and transfer into a salad bowl, then core and chop the apples and add them to the salad bowl with the chopped scallions and celery.

2 Add the Mayonnaise and season to taste with salt and pepper. Stir well to mix, then let cool and stand so the flavors develop. Serve at room temperature.

arugula & avocado salad

cook: 0 mins   **prep: 15 mins**   **serves 6**

This is a salad of contrasts—bitter arugula, sharp walnuts, and tangy red onions set against refreshing orange, crisp lettuce, and buttery, rich avocado. The huge variety of colors and flavors will whet the appetite and set your taste buds tingling. The salad is suitable for both vegetarians and vegans.

variation

For a milder nutty flavor, substitute ½ cup of toasted pine nuts for the chopped walnuts, if you prefer.

INGREDIENTS

1 red or green escarole lettuce, torn
½ frisée lettuce, torn
1 small bunch of watercress or mizuna
1 bunch of arugula, torn
1 red onion, thinly sliced into rings
2 oranges
1 avocado
½ cup coarsely chopped walnuts

DRESSING

6 tbsp olive oil
1 tbsp walnut oil
3 tbsp lemon juice
2 tbsp orange juice
1 tsp finely grated orange rind
1 tsp Dijon mustard
pinch of sugar
salt and pepper

cook's tip

Always make sure that salad greens are well dried after washing. Use a salad spinner, except for delicate greens, or pat dry gently with paper towels or a dish towel.

1 To make the dressing, place all the ingredients in a small bowl and whisk to mix. Season to taste with salt and pepper.

2 Place the lettuces, watercress, and arugula in a salad bowl and add the onion. Peel the oranges with a sharp knife and cut between the membranes to release the segments. Add the segments to the bowl.

3 Peel, pit, and dice the avocado and add to the salad. Pour over the dressing and toss well to coat. Sprinkle the walnuts over the top and serve immediately.

roast vegetable salad

serves 6   **prep: 25 mins** ⟳   **cook: 35 mins** 🖐

A colorful collection of Mediterranean vegetables makes a wonderful salad for a hot summer's day. A coating of olive oil adds richness to this satisfying dish, which is best served just warm, or at room temperature, with a few crusty bread rolls. The dish is suitable for both vegetarians and vegans.

INGREDIENTS

6 tbsp olive oil	3 red onions, cut into fourths
2 eggplants	6 plum tomatoes, cut into fourths
1 yellow bell pepper, seeded and cut into fourths	6 fresh basil leaves
1 red bell pepper, seeded and cut into fourths	DRESSING
1 orange bell pepper, seeded and cut into fourths	4 tbsp olive oil
	1 tbsp red wine vinegar
6 shallots	1 garlic clove, finely chopped
	salt and pepper

NUTRITIONAL INFORMATION

Calories	.249
Protein	.3g
Carbohydrate	.17g
Sugars	.14g
Fat	.19g
Saturates	.3g

variation

Root vegetables such as carrots and parsnips could be added to this roast. Baby carrots can be added whole, but cut larger vegetables into fourths.

cook's tip

Make sure that the vegetables are thoroughly coated in oil before placing them in the oven, otherwise they may dry out when roasting.

1 Preheat the oven to 450°F/230°C. Pour the oil into a large roasting pan. Add the eggplants, bell peppers, shallots, onions, and tomatoes and toss to coat. Roast in the preheated oven for 20 minutes, turning occasionally. Transfer the bell peppers, shallots, onions, and tomatoes to a serving platter with a perforated spoon.

2 Return the eggplants to the oven and roast, turning once, for an additional 15 minutes. Remove from the oven and let cool until cold enough to handle, then cut into bite-size pieces and add to the vegetable platter.

3 To make the dressing, mix the oil, vinegar, and garlic together, whisking well with a fork. Season to taste with salt and pepper and pour over the vegetables. Let cool until just warm, then sprinkle the vegetables with the basil leaves and serve.

cucumber & mushroom salad

serves 4 **prep: 10 mins,** plus 30 mins marinating **cook: 0 mins**

This easy-to-make salad is a useful, year-round accompaniment, versatile enough to go well with a wide variety of main meals. It is suitable for both vegetarians and vegans.

INGREDIENTS

½ cucumber cut into chunks
4 oz/115 g white mushrooms, sliced
1 small lettuce, torn
4 tomatoes, sliced
1 tbsp chopped fresh cilantro

DRESSING

2 tbsp olive oil
1 tbsp white wine vinegar
1 bay leaf
1 garlic clove, finely chopped
1 fresh tarragon sprig
1 fresh rosemary sprig
salt and pepper

NUTRITIONAL INFORMATION

Calories	.74
Protein	.2g
Carbohydrate	.4g
Sugars	.3g
Fat	.6g
Saturates	.1g

cook's tip

To clean mushrooms, wipe with damp paper towels or brush with a small vegetable brush. With the exception of morels, mushrooms should not be immersed in water.

1 To make the dressing, place the oil, vinegar, bay leaf, garlic, tarragon, and rosemary in a large bowl and whisk well. Season to taste with salt and pepper. Add the cucumber and mushrooms, tossing well to mix. Cover with plastic wrap and let marinate for 30 minutes.

2 Place the lettuce in a salad bowl. Transfer the mushrooms and cucumber to the bowl with a perforated spoon and add the tomatoes. Sprinkle with the cilantro.

3 Strain the dressing and discard the herbs. Pour over the salad and serve.

mixed bean salad

cook: 10 mins   **prep: 10 mins**   **serves 4**

This is the perfect side dish to accompany burgers for a barbecue grill, but it also makes a good combination when served with pies and quiches. It is suitable for both vegetarians and vegans.

NUTRITIONAL INFORMATION

Calories 200

Protein 8g

Carbohydrate 23g

Sugars 9g

Fat 9g

Saturates 1g

INGREDIENTS

4 oz/115 g green beans

2 celery stalks, chopped

2 shallots, chopped

3 tomatoes, chopped

15 oz/425 g canned mixed beans, drained and rinsed

3 tbsp chopped fresh parsley

DRESSING

3 tbsp olive oil

1 tbsp red wine vinegar

1 garlic clove, finely chopped

1 tbsp tomato chutney

salt and pepper

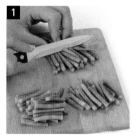

cook's tip

It is best to use precooked, canned beans for salads, to save time and energy that would otherwise be spent soaking and boiling them.

1 Steam the beans over a pan of boiling water for 10 minutes, or until tender. Remove from the heat, refresh under cold running water, drain, and cut in half.

2 Meanwhile, make the dressing. Place the oil, vinegar, garlic, and tomato chutney in a bowl and whisk well. Season to taste with salt and pepper.

3 Put the beans, celery, shallots, tomatoes, and mixed beans into a salad bowl. Add the dressing and toss well. Sprinkle with the parsley and serve immediately.

caesar salad

serves 4   **prep: 15 mins,** plus 20 mins cooling   **cook: 20 mins**

Caesar Cardini, not Caesar Augustus, created this salad at his restaurant in Tijuana, Mexico, in the 1920s. The dish is now regarded as a classic, and often appears on restaurant menus.

INGREDIENTS

1 garlic clove, halved

1 romaine lettuce

½ cup coarsely grated Parmesan cheese

GARLIC CROUTONS

3 tbsp olive oil

1 large garlic clove, halved

4 slices whole-wheat bread, crusts removed, cut into cubes

DRESSING

1 egg

1 tsp vegetarian Worcestershire sauce

2 tbsp lemon juice

2 tsp Dijon mustard

2 tbsp olive oil

salt and pepper

NUTRITIONAL INFORMATION

Calories	.280
Protein	.11g
Carbohydrate	.14g
Sugars	.2g
Fat	.21g
Saturates	.5g

variation

Add a pinch of cayenne pepper and 1 teaspoon of paprika to the oil when you make the croutons in Step 1.

cook's tip

For children, invalids, and pregnant women, omit the lightly cooked egg from the dressing and add hard-cooked eggs, cut into fourths.

1 Preheat the oven to 375°F/190°C. To make the croutons, pour the oil into a small pan and add the garlic. Heat gently for 5 minutes. Remove and discard the garlic. Place the cubes of bread in a bowl and pour in the oil. Toss to coat, then spread the cubes out on a cookie sheet. Bake in the preheated oven for

10 minutes, or until crisp. Remove from the oven and let cool.

2 To make the dressing, place the egg in a pan of water, bring to a boil, and continue boiling for 1 minute, then remove with a perforated spoon. Crack the egg into a bowl, scooping out any remaining egg white from

the shell. Whisk in the Worcestershire sauce, lemon juice, mustard, and oil and season with salt and pepper.

3 Rub the inside of a salad bowl with the halves of garlic, then discard. Arrange the lettuce leaves in the salad bowl and sprinkle with the Parmesan cheese. Drizzle the dressing over the

salad and sprinkle the garlic croutons on top. Toss the salad at the table and serve.

desserts

No meal is complete without a tempting dessert to round it off. Even the most
filling main dish will not dull the appetite for a light third course such as Toasted Tropical
Fruit (see page 252) or Citrus Meringue Crush (see page 251). If you long for something cooling
and fresh, you will find unusual and imaginative Winter Puddings (see page 226) or Chocolate
Honey Ice Cream (see page 253) difficult to resist—and if you are a chocolate addict, a feast of
delicious recipes awaits, from hot Chocolate Cranberry Sponge (see page 216) to a heavenly
Chocolate Brownie Roulade (see page 234) and nutty Chocolate Pecan Pie (see page 237).

On a cold evening, when you want a dessert that is filling and comforting,
warm crumbles and sponge bakes fit the bill perfectly. You'll love this section's Tropical Fruit
Crumble (see page 220), and for family gatherings, traditional Spiced Steamed Sponge (see page
219) and Bread & Butter Pudding (see page 228) always go down well. To tempt the children,
try Banana Cream Profiteroles (see page 238), Apple Fritters (see page 222), or Chocolate Cloud
(see page 240), and if you're looking for something a little different to surprise dinner party
guests, Traditional Tiramisù (see page 247) or Almond Cheesecakes (see page 244) are bound
to provide a talking point. If your guests stay overnight, you could serve a special treat with
mid-morning coffee, such as melt-in-the-mouth Carrot & Ginger Cake (see page 215) or
slices of Strawberry Roulade (see page 233).

carrot & ginger cake

⏱ **cook: 1 hr 15 mins**

⏱ **prep: 15 mins, plus 1 hr 20 mins cooling**

serves 10

This melt-in-the-mouth version of a favorite cake contains a fraction of the fat of the traditional version. It takes its texture and flavor from grated carrots, and after baking it is covered in delicious soft cheese, sweetened by vanilla extract and sugar.

variation

To make ordinary butter frosting, mix 6 tablespoons unsalted butter, 1¾ cups confectioners' sugar, and 1 teaspoon vanilla extract with a little water.

INGREDIENTS

butter, for greasing

generous 1½ cups all-purpose flour

1 tsp baking powder

1 tsp baking soda

2 tsp ground ginger

½ tsp salt

scant 1 cup light brown sugar

8 oz/225 g carrots, grated

2 pieces stem ginger in syrup, drained and chopped

1 oz/25 g grated fresh gingerroot

⅓ cup seedless raisins

2 eggs, beaten

3 tbsp corn oil

juice of 1 orange

FROSTING

8 oz/225 g lowfat soft cheese

4 tbsp confectioners' sugar

1 tsp vanilla extract

TO DECORATE

stem ginger pieces

freshly grated gingerroot

cook's tip

When you are making frosting, always beat the butter or soft cheese until smooth before adding the rest of the ingredients, otherwise they will not combine properly.

1 Preheat the oven to 350°F/180°C. Grease and line an 8-inch/20-cm round cake pan with parchment paper.

2 Sift the flour, baking powder, baking soda, ground ginger, and salt together into a large bowl. Stir in the sugar, carrots, stem ginger, gingerroot, and raisins.

Beat the eggs, oil, and orange juice together, then add to the flour mixture and mix well.

3 Spoon the mixture into the prepared cake pan and bake in the preheated oven for 1–1¼ hours, or until firm to the touch and a skewer inserted into the center of the cake comes out clean. Let cool in the pan.

4 To make the frosting, place the soft cheese in a bowl and beat to soften. Strain in the confectioners' sugar and add the vanilla extract. Mix well. Remove the cake from the pan and smooth the frosting over the top. Decorate with pieces of stem ginger and a little grated fresh gingerroot, then serve.

chocolate cranberry sponge

serves 4   **prep: 20 mins**   **cook: 1 hr**

The sharpness and freshness of a fruity cranberry and apple topping contrasts deliciously with the sweetness of the chocolate in this wonderful, fluffy sponge dessert. Served with a thick, creamy, dark chocolate sauce, it makes a special mouthwatering treat to round off a perfect meal.

INGREDIENTS

4 tbsp unsalted butter, plus extra for greasing

4 tbsp dark brown sugar, plus extra for sprinkling

generous ¾ cup cranberries, thawed if frozen

1 large cooking apple

2 eggs, lightly beaten

⅔ cup self-rising flour

3 tbsp unsweetened cocoa

SAUCE

6 oz/175 g semisweet chocolate, broken into pieces

1¾ cups evaporated milk

1 tsp vanilla extract

½ tsp almond extract

NUTRITIONAL INFORMATION

Calories 733

Protein 17g

Carbohydrate 74g

Sugars 55g

Fat 43g

Saturates 26g

variation

For a slightly richer chocolate sauce, replace the evaporated milk with heavy cream, stirring it in after the chocolate has melted in Step 3.

cook's tip

For the best result when making the chocolate sauce, it is best to use good-quality semisweet chocolate, made from 70 per cent cocoa solids.

1 Grease a 5-cup ovenproof bowl, sprinkle with sugar to coat the sides, and tip out any excess. Place the cranberries in a separate bowl. Using a sharp knife, peel, core, and dice the apple, then mix with the cranberries and place in the prepared ovenproof bowl.

2 Place the butter, brown sugar, and eggs in a large bowl. Sift in the flour and cocoa and beat until mixed. Pour into the ovenproof bowl over the fruit, cover the top with foil, and tie with string. Place the bowl in a steamer set over a large pan of simmering water and steam for 1 hour, or until risen, topping up with boiling water, if necessary.

3 Meanwhile, make the sauce. Place the chocolate and milk in the top of a double boiler or in a heatproof bowl set over a pan of barely simmering water. Stir until the chocolate has melted, then remove from the heat. Whisk in the vanilla and almond extracts and beat until thick and smooth.

4 To serve, remove the ovenproof bowl from the heat and discard the foil. Run a spatula around the inside of the bowl, place a serving plate on top of the sponge and, holding them together, invert. Serve immediately, with the sauce.

spiced steamed sponge

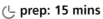

 cook: 1 hr 30 mins   **prep: 15 mins**   **serves 6**

variation

If you can't find ground cinnamon in your pantry, you can substitute allspice instead.

Steamed desserts are irresistible on a winter's day, but the texture of this sponge is so light it can be served throughout the year.

INGREDIENTS

2 tbsp corn syrup, plus extra to serve

generous ½ cup butter or vegetarian margarine

scant ⅔ cup superfine or light brown sugar

2 eggs

1¼ cups self-rising flour

¾ tsp ground cinnamon

grated rind of 1 orange

1 tbsp orange juice

½ cup golden raisins

1½ oz/40 g stem ginger, finely chopped

1 eating apple, peeled and cored

cook's tip

In Step 4, make a handle for the ovenproof bowl by tying a piece of string across the top of the bowl, anchored to the string holding the foil in place. This will make it easier to lift (see picture, left).

1 Thoroughly grease a 3½-cup ovenproof bowl. Place the corn syrup in the bowl.

2 Cream the butter and sugar together in a separate large bowl until the mixture is light, fluffy, and pale in color. Beat in the eggs, one at a time, following each with a spoonful of the flour.

3 Strain the remaining flour into the egg mixture with the ground cinnamon and fold in. Fold in the orange rind and juice, golden raisins, and ginger, then grate in the apple and stir gently to mix.

4 Spoon the mixture into the prepared ovenproof bowl and smooth the top.

Cover with a piece of pleated greased parchment paper, then cover with a sheet of pleated foil, folding around the edges of the bowl. Tie in place with string.

5 Place the bowl on a trivet in a pan and pour in enough boiling water to come halfway up the sides of the bowl. Cover and simmer

for 1½ hours, topping up with boiling water as necessary.

6 Remove the foil and parchment paper, turn the sponge on to a warmed serving plate, and serve with extra corn syrup.

tropical fruit crumble

serves 4　　　　**prep: 10 mins** 🕐　　　　**cook: 50 mins** 🕐

In this delicious crumble, fresh tropical fruits are flavored with ginger and coconut for a Caribbean-style dessert that is a little different—and extremely tasty.

INGREDIENTS

2 mangoes, sliced

1 papaya, seeded and sliced

8 oz/225 g fresh pineapple, cubed

1½ tsp ground ginger

scant ½ cup vegetarian margarine

½ cup light brown sugar

1¼ cups all-purpose flour

generous ½ cup dry unsweetened coconut, plus extra to decorate

NUTRITIONAL INFORMATION	
Calories	.602
Protein	.6g
Carbohydrate	.84g
Sugars	.51g
Fat	.29g
Saturates	.11g

variation

Use other fruits such as apples, blackberries, or plums for this dessert, and add chopped nuts to the topping instead of the unsweetened coconut.

1 Preheat the oven to 350°F/180°C. Place the mangoes, papaya, and pineapple in a pan with ½ teaspoon ground ginger, 2 tablespoons margarine, and half the sugar. Cook over low heat for 10 minutes, or until the fruit softens. Spoon the fruit into the bottom of a shallow ovenproof dish.

2 Place the flour and remaining ginger in a bowl and mix well. Add the remaining margarine and rub it in until the mixture resembles fine bread crumbs. Stir in the remaining sugar and coconut. Spoon over the fruit.

3 Cook the crumble in the preheated oven for 40 minutes, or until the top is crisp. Sprinkle over a little coconut to decorate and serve immediately.

rhubarb & apple crumble

cook: 45 mins **prep: 15 mins** **serves 6**

A mixture of tangy rhubarb and apples flavored with orange rind, brown sugar, and spices makes a delicious, warming dessert, which is topped with a crunchy, nutty crumble.

NUTRITIONAL INFORMATION	
Calories	.516
Protein	.6g
Carbohydrate	.77g
Sugars	.45g
Fat	.22g
Saturates	.4g

INGREDIENTS

1 lb 2 oz/500 g rhubarb

1 lb 2 oz/500 g tart cooking apples

grated rind and juice of 1 orange

½–1 tsp ground cinnamon

generous ⅓ cup light soft brown sugar

TOPPING

generous 1½ cups all-purpose flour

generous ½ cup butter or
vegan margarine

scant ⅔ cup light soft brown sugar

⅓ cup toasted chopped hazelnuts

2 tbsp dark brown sugar (optional)

cook's tip

When making a crumble, make sure that you do not overfill the dish with fruit. The dish should be two-thirds full of filling, to allow room for the crumble topping.

1 Preheat the oven to 400°F/200°C. Cut the rhubarb into 1-inch/2.5-cm lengths and place in a large pan.

2 Peel, core, and slice the apples and add to the rhubarb with the grated orange rind and juice. Bring to a boil, then reduce the heat and simmer for 2–3 minutes, or until the fruit begins to soften. Add the cinnamon and sugar to taste and spoon the mixture into an ovenproof dish.

3 To make the topping, strain the flour into a bowl. Add the butter and rub it in until the mixture resembles fine bread crumbs. Stir in the sugar, then the nuts. Spoon the mixture evenly over the fruit in the dish and smooth the top. Sprinkle with dark brown sugar, if you like.

4 Cook in the preheated oven for 30–40 minutes, or until the topping is golden brown. Serve hot or cold.

apple fritters

serves 4   **prep: 15 mins**   **cook: 15 mins**

These delicious apple fritters are coated in a light, spiced batter and deep-fried until they are crisp and golden. They are served warm with an unusual almond sauce.

INGREDIENTS

¾ cup all-purpose flour	vegetable or corn oil,
salt	for deep-frying
½ tsp ground cinnamon, plus extra	1 tbsp superfine sugar, to decorate
to decorate	
¾ cup warm water	SAUCE
4 tsp vegetable oil	⅔ cup plain yogurt
2 egg whites	½ tsp almond extract
2 eating apples, peeled	2 tsp clear honey

NUTRITIONAL INFORMATION

Calories	.538
Protein	.6g
Carbohydrate	.35g
Sugars	.15g
Fat	.32g
Saturates	.4g

variation

Try cooking chunks of banana in the batter as a substitute for, or in addition to, the chunks of apple.

cook's tip

Make sure the oil is very hot before you begin cooking the fritters, otherwise they may turn out soggy rather than light and crisp.

1 Strain the flour and a pinch of salt into a large bowl, then add the ground cinnamon and mix well. Stir in the warm water and vegetable oil to make a smooth batter.

2 Whisk the egg whites in a spotlessly clean, greasefree bowl until stiff peaks form, then gently fold into the batter. Using a sharp knife, cut the apples into even-size chunks.

3 Heat the oil for deep-frying to 350–375°F/ 180–190°C, or until a teaspoon of batter dropped into the oil rises immediately to the surface. Dip the apple chunks into the batter to coat, then cook, in batches if necessary, for 3–4 minutes, or until light golden and puffy. Remove the with a perforated spoon and drain on paper towels.

4 Mix the superfine sugar and a little ground cinnamon together and sprinkle over the fritters. Mix the sauce ingredients together in a small serving bowl and serve with the fritters.

summer fruit clafoutis

cook: 50 mins

prep: 15 mins, plus 1 hr 30 mins chilling/standing

serves 4

NUTRITIONAL INFORMATION

Calories	228
Protein	9g
Carbohydrate	42g
Sugars	26g
Fat	2g
Saturates	1g

variation

Other fruits that work just as well in this clafoutis include fresh blackberries, cherries, gooseberries, red currants, and black currants.

Serve this mouthwatering French-style fruit-in-batter dessert hot or cold, with a helping of mascarpone or plain yogurt.

INGREDIENTS

1 lb 2 oz/500 g prepared fresh assorted soft fruits, such as blueberries, raspberries, and strawberries

4 tbsp soft fruit liqueur, such as crème de cassis, kirsch, or framboise

4 tbsp skim milk powder

scant 1 cup all-purpose flour

salt

¼ cup superfine sugar

2 eggs, beaten

1¼ cups skim milk

1 tsp vanilla extract

2 tsp superfine sugar, for dusting

TO SERVE

assorted soft fruits

lowfat plain yogurt

or mascarpone

cook's tip

Chilling the fruit for 1 hour lets it macerate, or soften. This is important for the finished texture of the clafoutis, which should slice through easily.

1 Place the assorted fruits in a bowl and spoon over the fruit liqueur. Cover and chill in the refrigerator for 1 hour.

2 Preheat the oven to 400°F/200°C. Mix the milk powder, flour, a pinch of salt, and the sugar together in a large bowl. Make a well in the center and, using a balloon whisk, gradually whisk in the eggs, milk, and vanilla extract until smooth. Transfer to a pitcher and let stand for 30 minutes. Line the bottom of a 9-inch/23-cm round ovenproof baking dish with parchment paper and spoon in the fruits and juices.

3 Re-whisk the batter and pour over the fruits in the ovenproof dish. Stand the dish on a cookie sheet, then bake in the preheated oven for 50 minutes, or until firm, risen, and golden brown. Dust with superfine sugar. Serve with extra fruits, lowfat plain yogurt, or mascarpone.

winter puddings

serves 4 **prep: 25 mins, plus 8 hrs 20 mins cooling/chilling** **cook: 10 mins**

This recipe uses dried fruits and a tasty malt loaf to create an interesting alternative to the traditional English summer pudding.

INGREDIENTS

11½ oz/325 g fruit malt loaf

5½ oz/150 g no-soak dried apricots, coarsely chopped

3 oz/85 g dried apple, coarsely chopped

generous 1¾ cups orange juice

1 tsp grated orange rind, plus extra to decorate

2 tbsp orange liqueur

lowfat sour cream or mascarpone, to serve

NUTRITIONAL INFORMATION

Calories	.447
Protein	.9g
Carbohydrate	.80g
Sugars	.68g
Fat	.11g
Saturates	.5g

variation

You could add 1 tablespoon of raisins or golden raisins to the fruit before cooking in Step 1, if you like.

cook's tip

Choose plump, sun-dried apricots for this dish, because they do not need soaking. They will taste moist and juicy in the finished puddings.

1 Cut the malt loaf into ½-inch/1-cm slices. Place the apricots, apple, and orange juice in a pan. Bring to a boil, then reduce the heat and simmer for 10 minutes. Using a perforated spoon, remove the fruit and reserve the liquid. Place the fruit in a dish and let cool. Stir in the orange rind and liqueur.

2 Line 4 x ¾-cup ovenproof bowls or ramekins with parchment paper.

3 Cut 4 circles from the malt loaf slices to fit the tops of the bowls, then cut the remaining slices into pieces small enough to line them. Soak the malt loaf slices in the reserved fruit syrup, then arrange around the bottom and sides of the bowls. Trim away any overhanging crusts. Fill the center with the fruit, pressing down well, and place the malt loaf circles on top.

4 Cover with parchment paper and weigh each bowl down with an 8-oz/225-g weight or a food can. Chill in the refrigerator for at least 8 hours.

5 Remove the weight and parchment paper. Carefully turn the puddings out on to serving plates and remove the lining paper. Decorate with orange rind and serve with sour cream or mascarpone.

bread & butter pudding

serves 4 **prep: 20 mins, plus** 🕛 **10 mins standing/cooling** **cook: 35–45 mins** 🕒

Brioche gives this traditional dessert a lovely rich flavor, but this recipe also works well with soft-baked batch bread.

INGREDIENTS

8 oz/225 g brioche

1 tbsp butter

1¾ oz/50 g semisweet chocolate chips

1 egg

2 egg yolks

4 tbsp superfine sugar

generous 1¾ cups lowfat evaporated milk

NUTRITIONAL INFORMATION	
Calories	.440
Protein	.17g
Carbohydrate	.60g
Sugars	.33g
Fat	.16g
Saturates	.33g

variation

For a double-chocolate pudding, heat the milk with 1 tablespoon unsweetened cocoa in Step 4, stirring until well dissolved.

1 Preheat the oven to 350°F/180°C. Cut the brioche into thin slices. Lightly butter one side of each slice. Place a layer of brioche, buttered-side down, in the bottom of a shallow ovenproof dish. Sprinkle over a few chocolate chips. Continue layering the brioche and chocolate chips, finishing with a layer of bread.

2 Whisk the egg, egg yolks, and sugar together until blended. Heat the milk in a small pan until it just begins to simmer, then gradually add to the egg mixture, whisking well.

3 Pour the custard over the pudding and let stand for 5 minutes. Press the brioche into the liquid.

4 Place the pudding in a roasting pan and fill with boiling water to come halfway up the sides of the dish. Bake in the preheated oven for 30 minutes, or until the custard has set. Let cool for 5 minutes before serving.

ginger & apricot alaskas

cook: 10 mins   **prep: 15 mins**   **serves 2**

There is no ice cream in these Alaskas, but a mixture of apples and apricots poached in orange juice is enclosed in the sweet meringue.

NUTRITIONAL INFORMATION

Calories	.442
Protein	.7g
Carbohydrate	.83g
Sugars	.77g
Fat	.9g
Saturates	.3g

INGREDIENTS

2 slices rich, dark ginger cake,
about ¾-inch/2-cm thick

1–2 tbsp ginger wine or rum

1 eating apple

6 no-soak dried apricots, chopped

4 tbsp orange juice or water

1 tbsp slivered almonds

2 small egg whites

½ cup superfine sugar

variation

A slice of ice cream can be placed on the fruit before adding the meringue, but do this at the last minute, and eat the desserts immediately after cooking.

1 Preheat the oven to 400°F/200°C. Place the ginger cake slices on an ovenproof plate and sprinkle with the ginger wine or rum.

2 Cut the apple into fourths, core it, and slice it into a small pan. Add the chopped apricots and orange juice or water and simmer over low heat for

5 minutes, or until tender. Stir the almonds into the fruit and spoon the mixture equally over the slices of soaked cake, piling it up in the center.

 3 Whisk the egg whites in a spotlessly clean, greasefree bowl until stiff peaks form, then whisk in the sugar, a little at a time, until the mixture is thick and glossy.

Continue whisking until all the sugar has been incorporated and the meringue is thick, white, and stands in tall peaks.

4 Pipe or spread the meringue over the fruit and cake to cover. Cook in the preheated oven for 4–5 minutes, or until golden brown. Serve immediately.

fruity crêpe bundles

cook: 35 mins

prep: 15 mins, plus 15 mins cooling

serves 2

variation

You can substitute other ready-to-eat dried fruit for the apricots, if you like, to create a slightly different filling.

These crêpes are filled with a sweet cream flavored with ginger, nuts, and apricots, and served with a raspberry and orange sauce.

INGREDIENTS

BATTER	
6 tbsp all-purpose flour	1 egg
salt	⅔ cup milk
¼ tsp ground cinnamon	scant ¼ cup chopped nuts
1 egg	1½ oz/40 g no-soak dried
scant ⅔ cup milk	apricots, chopped
1–2 tbsp white vegetable fat	1 piece candied ginger, finely chopped

FILLING	SAUCE
1½ tsp all-purpose flour, strained	3 tbsp raspberry jelly
1½ tsp cornstarch	4½ tsp orange juice
1 tbsp superfine sugar	finely grated rind of ¼ orange

cook's tip

To make thin, crispy crêpes, rock the skillet as you pour the batter in to make sure that it spreads out as thinly as possible. The secret to successful crêpes is very hot fat and quick cooking.

1 Preheat the oven to 350°F/180°C. To make the batter, strain the flour, a pinch of salt, and the cinnamon into a bowl and make a well in the center. Add the egg and milk and beat in gradually until smooth.

2 Melt the vegetable fat in a skillet. Pour in enough batter to cover the bottom thinly. Cook for 2 minutes, or until golden, then cook the other side for 1 minute, until browned. Transfer to a plate and cook another crêpe.

3 To make the filling, beat the flour, cornstarch, sugar, and egg together in a bowl. Heat the milk gently, then beat 2 tablespoons of it into the flour mixture. Transfer to the pan and cook gently, stirring, until thick. Remove from the heat, cover with parchment paper to prevent a skin forming, and cool.

4 Beat the nuts, apricots, and ginger into the mixture and put a heaped tablespoonful in the center of each crêpe. Gather and squeeze the edges together to make bundles. Place in an ovenproof dish and bake in the oven for 15–20 minutes, or until hot but not too brown.

5 To make the sauce, melt the jelly with the orange juice, then strain. Return to a clean pan with the orange rind and heat through. Serve with the crêpes.

brown sugar pavlovas

serves 4 **prep: 10 mins, plus 1hr 10 mins cooling** **cook: 55 mins**

This simple combination of fudgy meringue topped with mascarpone and raspberries is the perfect finale to any meal.

INGREDIENTS

2 large egg whites

1 tsp cornstarch

1 tsp raspberry vinegar

½ cup light brown sugar, crushed free of lumps

2 tbsp red currant jelly

2 tbsp unsweetened orange juice

⅔ cup lowfat mascarpone

6 oz/175 g raspberries, thawed if frozen

rose-scented geranium leaves, to decorate (optional)

NUTRITIONAL INFORMATION

Calories	155
Protein	5g
Carbohydrate	35g
Sugars	34g
Fat	0.2g
Saturates	0g

cook's tip

Make a large pavlova by forming the meringue into a single circle, 7 inches/18 cm across, on a lined cookie sheet, and bake in the preheated oven for 1 hour.

1 Preheat the oven to 300°F/150°C. Line a large cookie sheet with parchment paper. Whisk the egg whites in a spotlessly clean, greasefree bowl until stiff peaks form. Fold in the cornstarch and vinegar.

2 Gradually whisk in the sugar, a spoonful at a time, until the mixture is thick and glossy. Divide the mixture into 4 and spoon on to the cookie sheet, spaced well apart. Smooth each into a circle, 4 inches/10 cm across, and bake in the preheated oven for 40–45 minutes, or until lightly browned and crisp. Let cool on the cookie sheet.

3 Place the red currant jelly and orange juice in a small pan and heat gently, stirring constantly, until melted. Remove the pan from the heat and let cool for 10 minutes.

4 Using a spatula, remove the Pavlovas from the parchment paper and transfer to individual serving plates. Spoon over the mascarpone and scatter over the raspberries. Glaze with the red currant jelly and decorate with geranium leaves, if you like.

strawberry roulade

cook: 10 mins　　**prep: 30 mins, plus 20 mins cooling**　　**serves 8**

Serve this moist, light sponge rolled up with an almond and strawberry mascarpone filling for a delicious mid-afternoon treat.

NUTRITIONAL INFORMATION	
Calories	166
Protein	6g
Carbohydrate	30g
Sugars	19g
Fat	3g
Saturates	1g

INGREDIENTS

butter, for greasing

3 large eggs

scant ⅔ cup superfine sugar

scant 1 cup all-purpose flour

1 tbsp hot water

1 tbsp slivered toasted almonds

1 tsp confectioners' sugar

FILLING

generous ¾ cup lowfat mascarpone

1 tsp almond extract

8 oz/225 g small strawberries

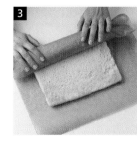

cook's tip

To line a jelly roll pan, use a single sheet of parchment paper, which overhangs the sides by 3 inches/7.5 cm. Press it into the pan and cut and fold down each corner to make it fit neatly.

1 Preheat the oven to 425°F/220°C. Line a 14 x 10-inch/35 x 25-cm jelly roll pan with parchment paper and grease.

2 Place the eggs in a large bowl with the superfine sugar. Place the bowl over a pan of hot water and whisk until pale and thick, then remove the bowl from the pan. Strain in the flour and fold into the egg mixture with the hot water. Pour the mixture into the pan and bake in the preheated oven for 8–10 minutes, or until golden and set.

3 Transfer the baked mixture to a sheet of parchment paper. Carefully peel off the lining paper, then roll up the sponge tightly, along with the parchment paper. Wrap the rolled sponge in a dish towel and let cool.

4 To make the filling, mix the mascarpone and almond extract together. Reserving a few strawberries for decoration, wash, hull, and slice the rest. Chill the mixture until required.

5 Unroll the sponge, spread the mascarpone mixture over it, and sprinkle with strawberries. Roll the sponge up again and transfer to a serving plate. Sprinkle with almonds and lightly dust with confectioners' sugar. Decorate with the reserved strawberries and serve.

chocolate brownie roulade

serves 8   **prep: 30 mins, plus 1 hr cooling**   **cook: 25 mins**

The addition of nuts and raisins has given this dessert extra texture, making it similar to that of chocolate brownies.

INGREDIENTS

butter, for greasing

5½ oz/150 g semisweet chocolate, broken into pieces

3 tbsp water

generous ¾ cup superfine sugar

5 eggs, separated

scant ¼ cup raisins, chopped

¼ cup pecans, chopped

salt

confectioners' sugar, for dusting

1¼ cups heavy cream, lightly whipped

variation

The chopped pecans can be substituted with another chopped nut of your choice, such as walnuts.

cook's tip

For the best results, make sure that you choose a good-quality semisweet chocolate with 70 per cent cocoa solids for this recipe.

1 Preheat the oven to 350°F/180°C. Grease a 12 x 8-inch/30 x 20-cm jelly roll pan, line with parchment paper, and grease.

2 Place the chocolate and water in a small pan and heat gently, stirring constantly, until the chocolate has just melted. Let cool.

3 Place the sugar and egg yolks in a bowl and whisk until thick and pale, then fold in the cooled chocolate, raisins, and pecans.

4 In a separate bowl, whisk the egg whites with a pinch of salt. Fold one fourth of the egg whites into the chocolate mixture, then fold in the rest of the whites,

lightly and quickly. Transfer the mixture into the pan and bake for 25 minutes, until risen and firm to the touch. Let cool, then cover with a sheet of nonstick parchment paper and a damp, clean dish towel. Let stand until cold.

5 Turn the roulade out onto parchment paper dusted with confectioners'

sugar and remove the lining paper. Spread the whipped cream over the roulade. Starting from a short end, roll the sponge away from you using the paper to guide you. Trim the ends of the roulade to make a neat finish and transfer to a serving plate. Chill in the refrigerator until ready to serve. Dust with a little confectioners' sugar before serving, if desired.

chocolate pecan pie

cook: 1 hr 15 mins

prep: 40 mins, plus 2 hrs chilling/cooling

serves 8

This classic American dessert is packed with deliciously contrasting flavors and textures and is simply irresistible.

INGREDIENTS

DOUGH	FILLING
2 cups all-purpose flour, plus extra for dusting	3 oz/85 g semisweet chocolate, broken into small pieces
6 tbsp unsweetened cocoa	12 oz/350 g shelled pecans
generous 1 cup confectioners' sugar	6 tbsp unsalted butter
salt	generous ¾ cup brown sugar
scant 1 cup unsalted butter, diced	3 eggs
1 egg yolk	2 tbsp heavy cream
	2 tbsp all-purpose flour
	1 tbsp confectioners' sugar, for dusting

variation

Pipe decorative florets of whipped heavy cream in between the pecans on top of the pie instead of dusting with confectioners' sugar, if you like.

cook's tip

When baking a tart shell blind, spread the dried beans evenly across the whole of the shell, otherwise air bubbles may form underneath the dough, making it uneven.

1 Preheat the oven to 350°F/180°C. To make the dough, sift the flour, cocoa, sugar, and a pinch of salt into a bowl. Make a well in the center, add the butter and egg yolk, and mix. Knead into a ball, wrap in plastic wrap, and chill for 1 hour. Unwrap the dough, roll out on a lightly floured counter, and use it to line a 10-inch/25-cm nonstick springform tart pan. Prick the bottom with a fork. Line with parchment paper, fill with dried beans, and bake for 15 minutes. Remove from the oven, discard the beans and paper, and let cool.

2 Place the chocolate in a heatproof bowl set over a pan of simmering water until melted. Remove from the heat and reserve. Chop 8 oz/225 g pecans and reserve. Mix the butter with ¼ cup brown sugar. Beat in the eggs, one at a time, then mix in the remaining brown sugar. Stir in the cream, flour, chocolate, and chopped pecan nuts. Spoon into the tart shell and smooth the surface. Arrange the remaining pecans over the pie.

3 Bake in the preheated oven for 30 minutes, then remove the pie and cover the top with foil to prevent it burning. Bake for an additional 25 minutes. Remove the pie from the oven and let cool slightly before removing it from the pan and transferring to a wire rack to cool completely. Dust the pie with confectioners' sugar and serve.

banana cream profiteroles

serves 4   **prep: 20 mins, plus**   **cook: 30 mins**
30 mins cooling

Chocolate profiteroles are a popular choice for a special dessert. In this recipe they are filled with a thoroughly delicious banana-flavored cream—the perfect combination!

INGREDIENTS

CHOUX PASTRY

5 tbsp butter, plus extra for greasing

⅔ cup water

⅔ cup all-purpose flour, strained

2 eggs

FILLING

1¼ cups heavy cream

1 banana

2 tbsp confectioners' sugar

2 tbsp banana-flavored liqueur

CHOCOLATE SAUCE

3½ oz/100 g bittersweet chocolate, broken into pieces

2 tbsp water

4 tbsp confectioners' sugar

2 tbsp unsalted butter

NUTRITIONAL INFORMATION

Calories 890

Protein 9g

Carbohydrate 63g

Sugars 45g

Fat 68g

Saturates 42g

variation

For a banana and almond filling, substitute almond liqueur for the banana liqueur in Step 4.

cook's tip

Profiteroles look wonderful stacked in a pyramid. Build them up in smaller and smaller layers, then pour the chocolate sauce over the pyramid.

1 Preheat the oven to 425°F/220°C. Grease a cookie sheet and sprinkle with a little water. To make the choux pastry, place the water and butter in a pan and heat gently until the butter melts, then bring to a rolling boil. Remove the pan from the heat. Add the flour all at once and beat vigorously with a wooden spoon until the

mixture is smooth and comes away from the sides of the pan. Cool slightly, then gradually beat in the eggs until smooth and glossy. Spoon the paste into a large pastry bag fitted with a ½-inch/1-cm plain nozzle.

2 Pipe 18 small balls of the paste on to the cookie sheet, allowing room

for expansion during cooking. Bake in the preheated oven for 15–20 minutes, or until crisp and golden. Remove from the oven and make a small slit in each profiterole for steam to escape. Transfer to a wire rack to cool.

3 Meanwhile, make the sauce. Place all the ingredients in a heatproof

bowl set over a pan of simmering water and heat, stirring, until smooth. Reserve.

4 To make the filling, whip the cream into soft peaks. Mash the banana with the sugar and liqueur. Fold into the cream. Place in a pastry bag with a ½-inch/1-cm plain nozzle, pipe into the pastries, pour over the sauce, and serve.

chocolate cloud

This unbelievably easy, but deliciously memorable dessert can be made in a matter of a few minutes.

INGREDIENTS

4 oz/115 g semisweet chocolate,
broken into pieces

4 eggs, separated

2½ cups heavy cream

toasted slivered almonds,
to decorate

NUTRITIONAL INFORMATION

Calories	.600
Protein	.7g
Carbohydrate	.15g
Sugars	.14g
Fat	.57g
Saturates	.34g

variation

For a little extra richness, sprinkle a handful of chocolate chips over the top of the chocolate clouds with the almonds in Step 4.

1 Place the chocolate in the top of a double boiler or in a heatproof bowl set over a pan of barely simmering water and stir until melted. Remove from the heat and cool slightly, then beat in the egg yolks.

2 Whisk the egg whites in a spotlessly clean, greasefree bowl until stiff

peaks form, then fold them into the chocolate mixture. Let the mixture stand for 30 minutes, until beginning to set.

3 Whip 1¼ cups of the heavy cream until thick. Fold half of the whipped cream into the chocolate mixture, then spoon half of the mixture into 6 sundae glasses. Divide

the other half of the whipped cream between the glasses in a layer over the chocolate mixture. Top with the remaining chocolate mixture. Cover with plastic wrap and chill in the refrigerator for 30 minutes.

4 Just before serving, whip the remaining cream until thick. Pipe a swirl

of cream on the top of each dessert and sprinkle with a few toasted slivered almonds.

lemon & lime syllabub

cook: 0 mins

prep: 15 mins, plus 4 hrs infusing/chilling

serves 4

This dessert is rich, but absolutely mouthwatering. It is not for the calorie conscious, as it contains a high proportion of cream.

NUTRITIONAL INFORMATION

Calories 403

Protein 2g

Carbohydrate 16g

Sugars 16g

Fat 36g

Saturates 22g

INGREDIENTS

¼ cup superfine sugar

grated rind and juice of 1 small lemon

grated rind and juice of 1 small lime

scant ¼ cup Marsala wine

1¼ cups heavy cream

lime and lemon rind, to decorate

cook's tip

If you cannot find a bottle of the sweet Sicilian dessert wine, Marsala, the same amount of medium sherry will work almost as well.

1 Place the sugar, lemon juice and rind, lime juice and rind, and Marsala in a bowl. Mix well and let stand for 2 hours to infuse.

2 Add the cream to the fruit juice mixture and whisk until it just holds its shape, then spoon the mixture into 4 tall serving glasses and chill in the refrigerator for 2 hours. Decorate with lime and lemon rind and serve.

lime cheesecakes

cook: 5 mins

prep: 30 mins, plus 2 hrs chilling

serves 2

These cheesecakes are flavored with lime and mint, and set on a mixture of crushed graham crackers and chocolate.

NUTRITIONAL INFORMATION

Calories 696

Protein 18g

Carbohydrate 70g

Sugars 44g

Fat 40g

Saturates 22g

variation

Beat 1 finely chopped sprig of fresh mint into the cheese mixture in Step 3 for a little extra flavor, if you like.

INGREDIENTS

SHELLS

2 tbsp butter, plus extra for greasing

1 oz/25 g semisweet chocolate

3 oz/85 g crushed graham crackers

FILLING

finely grated rind of 1 lime

generous ⅓ cup curd cheese

generous ⅓ cup lowfat soft cheese

1 tsp vegetarian gelatin

1 tbsp lime juice

1 egg yolk

scant ¼ cup superfine sugar

TO DECORATE

whipped cream

kiwi fruit slices

fresh mint sprigs

cook's tip

To melt the chocolate in a microwave in Step 1, place the bowl of butter and chocolate inside the cooker and microwave on High power for about 1 minute.

1 Grease 2 fluted, loose-bottomed 4½-inch/12-cm tart pans. To make the shells, melt the butter and chocolate in a heatproof bowl set over a pan of gently simmering water. Stir until smooth. Stir the crushed graham crackers evenly through the melted chocolate, then press into the bottom of the tart pans and smooth the surfaces. Chill the graham cracker shells in the refrigerator for 1 hour, or until set.

2 To make the filling, place the grated lime rind and cheeses into a bowl. and beat until smooth and blended. Dissolve the gelatin in the lime juice in a separate heatproof bowl set over a pan of simmering water.

3 Place the egg yolk and sugar in a bowl and beat until creamy. Fold into the cheese mixture, then fold in the gelatin mixture. Pour over the graham cracker shells and chill in the refrigerator for 1 hour, or until set, then remove the cheesecakes from the tart pans, decorate with whipped cream, kiwi fruit, and fresh mint sprigs, and serve.

almond cheesecakes

serves 4 **prep: 20 mins, plus 1 hr 30 mins cooling/chilling** **cook: 10 mins**

These creamy almond-cheese desserts are so incredibly delicious, it's hard to believe that they are low in fat.

INGREDIENTS

12 amaretti cookies

1 egg white, lightly beaten

1 cup skim milk soft cheese

½ tsp almond extract

½ tsp finely grated lime rind

scant ¼ cup ground almonds

2 tbsp superfine sugar

generous ⅓ cup golden raisins

2 tsp powdered gelatin

2 tbsp boiling water

2 tbsp lime juice

TO DECORATE

¼ cup toasted slivered almonds

strips of lime rind

NUTRITIONAL INFORMATION

Calories 361

Protein 16g

Carbohydrate 43g

Sugars 29g

Fat 15g

Saturates 4g

---

variation

If you don't like the texture of lime rind, you can omit it when you beat the cheesecake mixture in Step 3.

---

cook's tip

If you don't have any dough rings to use for the cookie shells, poached egg rings of the same diameter will work just as well.

1 Preheat the oven to 350°F/180°C. Place the cookies in a clean plastic bag, seal the bag, and use a rolling pin to crush them into small pieces. Place the crumbs in a bowl and bind together with the egg white.

2 Arrange 4 nonstick dough rings, 3½ inches/ 9 cm across, on a cookie sheet lined with parchment paper. Divide the cookie mixture into 4 equal portions and spoon into the rings, pressing down. Bake for 10 minutes, or until crisp. Cool in the rings.

3 Beat the soft cheese, almond extract, lime rind, ground almonds, sugar, and golden raisins together in a bowl until well mixed.

4 Dissolve the gelatin in the boiling water in a separate bowl, then stir in the lime juice. Fold into the cheese mixture, spoon the mixture over the cookie shells and smooth the surfaces. Chill in the refrigerator for 1 hour, or until set.

5 Loosen the almond cheesecakes from the rings with a small spatula and transfer to serving plates. Decorate with toasted slivered almonds and strips of lime rind and serve.

traditional tiramisù

🍲 **cook: 5 mins**

🕐 **prep: 20 mins,
plus 2–8 hrs chilling**

serves 6

This is a favorite Italian dessert flavored with coffee and almond liqueur. Its rich taste makes it ideal for a dinner party dessert.

INGREDIENTS

20–24 sponge fingers, about 5½ oz/150 g

2 tbsp cold black coffee

1 tbsp coffee extract

2 tbsp almond liqueur

4 egg yolks

scant ½ cup superfine sugar

few drops of vanilla extract

grated rind of ½ lemon

generous 1½ cups mascarpone cheese

2 tsp lemon juice

1 cup heavy cream

1 tbsp milk

¼ cup lightly toasted slivered almonds

2 tbsp unsweetened cocoa

1 tbsp confectioners' sugar

variation

You can substitute either brandy or Marsala wine for the almond liqueur, if you prefer a slightly different taste.

cook's tip

The almond liqueur that works well in this recipe is amaretto, which you can find in most major food stores and liquor stores.

1 Arrange almost half of the sponge fingers in the bottom of a serving dish. Place the black coffee, coffee extract, and almond liqueur in a bowl and mix. Sprinkle just over half of the mixture over the sponge fingers.

2 Place the egg yolks in a heatproof bowl with the sugar, vanilla extract, and lemon rind. Stand over a pan of gently simmering water and whisk until very thick and creamy and the whisk leaves a heavy trail when lifted from the bowl.

3 Place the mascarpone cheese in a separate bowl with the lemon juice and beat until smooth. Stir into the egg mixture, and when evenly blended, pour half of the mixture over the sponge fingers and spread out evenly.

4 Add another layer of sponge fingers, sprinkle with the remaining coffee mixture, then cover with the rest of the cheese and egg mixture. Chill in the refrigerator for at least 2 hours, preferably overnight.

5 Whip the cream and milk together until fairly stiff and spread or pipe over the dessert. Sprinkle with the slivered almonds, then strain an even layer of cocoa over the top to cover completely. Finally, strain a layer of confectioners' sugar over the cocoa and serve.

warm currants in cassis

Crème de cassis is a blackcurrant-based liqueur which comes from France and is an excellent flavoring for fruit dishes.

INGREDIENTS

12 oz/350 g black currants

8 oz/225 g red currants

¼ cup superfine sugar

grated rind and juice of 1 orange

2 tsp arrowroot

2 tbsp crème de cassis

1¼ cups heavy cream, whipped

fresh mint sprigs, to decorate

NUTRITIONAL INFORMATION

Calories	.202
Protein	.2g
Carbohydrate	.35g
Sugars	.35g
Fat	.6g
Saturates	.4g

1. Strip the currants from their stalks with a fork. Place in a pan, add the sugar and orange rind and juice, and heat gently until the sugar has completely dissolved. Bring the mixture to a boil, then reduce the heat and simmer gently for 5 minutes.

2. Sieve the currants, returning the juice to the pan. Blend the arrowroot with a little water into a paste and mix into the juice. Bring to a boil over medium heat and cook until thickened. Cool slightly, then stir in the crème de cassis.

3. Transfer the fruit to individual dishes, add a spoonful of whipped cream, and decorate with mint sprigs. Serve immediately.

cook's tip

Arrowroot is a starchy substance extracted from the roots of tropical plants, and is a useful way to thicken sauces made from thin juices.

baked pears in cinnamon

cook: 30 mins   **prep: 10 mins**   **serves 4**

This simple recipe is easy to prepare and cook but is deliciously warming. It is served hot on a pool of lowfat custard.

NUTRITIONAL INFORMATION

Calories	207
Protein	2g
Carbohydrate	37g
Sugars	35g
Fat	6g
Saturates	2g

INGREDIENTS

4 ripe pears

2 tbsp lemon juice

¼ cup light brown sugar

1 tsp ground cinnamon

¼ cup lowfat spread

scant 2 cups lowfat custard

strips of lemon rind, to decorate

variation

For alternative flavors, replace the cinnamon with ground allspice and spoon over some warmed dark rum to serve.

1 Preheat the oven to 400°F/200°C. Core and peel the pears, then slice in half lengthwise and brush all over with the lemon juice. Place the pears, cored-side down, in a small nonstick roasting pan.

2 Place the sugar, cinnamon, and lowfat spread in a small pan and heat gently, stirring constantly, until the sugar has melted. Keep the heat low to prevent too much water evaporating from the lowfat spread. Spoon the mixture over the pears, then bake in the preheated oven, occasionally spooning the sugar mixture over the fruit, for 20–25 minutes, or until the fruit is tender and golden.

3 Heat the custard until piping hot and spoon over 4 warmed dessert plates. Arrange 2 pear halves on each plate, decorate with strips of lemon rind, and serve.

citrus meringue crush

cook: 10 mins

prep: 15 mins, plus 2 hrs freezing

serves 4

NUTRITIONAL INFORMATION

Calories	.165
Protein	.5g
Carbohydrate	37g
Sugars	32g
Fat	.1g
Saturates	.0.4g

variation

Substitute rich Greek yogurt for the plain yogurt to give the meringue crush a richer consistency.

This is an excellent way to use up left-over meringue shells, and is very simple to prepare. Serve with a spoonful of tangy fruit sauce.

INGREDIENTS

8 ready-made meringue nests

1¼ cups lowfat plain yogurt

½ tsp finely grated orange rind

1 tsp finely grated lemon rind

½ tsp finely grated lime rind

2 tbsp orange liqueur or unsweetened orange juice

2 tbsp lemon juice

2 tbsp lime juice

3 tbsp water

2–3 tsp superfine sugar

1 tsp cornstarch

TO DECORATE

sliced kumquat

grated lime rind

FRUIT SAUCE

2 oz/55 g kumquats

½ cup unsweetened orange juice

cook's tip

To crush the meringue nests, rather than pummelling them with the rolling pin, place the rolling pin on top of them and press down with your full body weight.

1 Place the meringues in a plastic bag and crush with a rolling pin. Place in a bowl and stir in the yogurt, grated citrus rinds, and liqueur. Spoon the mixture into 4 small bowls and freeze for 1½–2 hours, or until firm.

2 To make the fruit sauce, thinly slice the kumquats and place in a small pan with the fruit juices and 2 tablespoons of the water. Bring gently to a boil, then simmer over low heat for 3–4 minutes, or until the kumquats soften.

3 Sweeten the sauce with sugar to taste. Mix the cornstarch with the remaining 1 tablespoon water, stir into the sauce and cook, stirring, until thickened. Pour into a small bowl, cover the surface with plastic wrap to prevent a skin forming, and let cool. Chill in the refrigerator until required.

4 To serve, dip the meringue bowls in hot water for 5 seconds, or until they loosen, and turn on to serving plates. Spoon over a little sauce, decorate with slices of kumquat and grated lime rind, and serve immediately.

toasted tropical fruit

serves 4   **prep: 20 mins, plus 30 mins soaking**   **cook: 5 mins**

For a tropical barbecue surprise, spear some chunks of colorful exotic fruit on to skewers, then sear them over hot coals or under the broiler and serve them with an amazing chocolate dip.

INGREDIENTS

1 mango

1 papaya

2 kiwi fruit

½ small pineapple

1 large banana

2 tbsp lemon juice

⅔ cup white rum

DIP

4½ oz/125 g semisweet chocolate pieces

2 tbsp corn syrup

1 tbsp unsweetened cocoa

1 tbsp cornstarch

generous ¾ cup milk

NUTRITIONAL INFORMATION	
Calories 435
Protein 6g
Carbohydrate 68g
Sugars 60g
Fat 11g
Saturates 6g

cook's tip

Keep the chunks of fruit fairly large. This makes them easy to thread on to the skewers, and makes them less likely to fall off during the cooking process.

1 Preheat the barbecue grill or broiler. To make the dip, place the chocolate, syrup, cocoa, cornstarch, and milk in a heavy-bottomed pan and heat gently, stirring, until thickened and smooth. Keep warm.

2 Slice the mango on each side of its large, flat stone. Cut the flesh into chunks, removing the peel. Halve, seed, and peel the papaya, then cut into chunks. Peel the kiwi fruit and slice into chunks. Peel the pineapple and cut into chunks. Peel and slice the banana and dip into the lemon juice.

3 Thread the pieces of fruit alternately on to 4 presoaked wooden skewers and place them in a shallow dish. Pour over the rum and let soak for 30 minutes.

4 Cook the kabobs over medium hot coals or under the broiler, turning frequently, for 2 minutes, or until seared. Serve with the hot chocolate dip.

chocolate honey ice cream

cook: 15 mins

prep: 30 mins, plus 5 hrs cooling/freezing

serves 6

Ice cream is always a popular summer dessert—try this rich, unusual recipe for a refreshing change, served with a few fresh strawberries, half-coated in semisweet chocolate.

NUTRITIONAL INFORMATION

Calories	365
Protein	9g
Carbohydrate	48g
Sugars	47g
Fat	17g
Saturates	9g

INGREDIENTS

generous 2 cups milk

7 oz/200 g semisweet chocolate, broken into pieces

4 eggs, separated

scant ½ cup superfine sugar

salt

2 tbsp clear honey

12 fresh strawberries, washed and hulled

cook's tip

The ice cream is transferred to the refrigerator for 10 minutes before serving to let it soften slightly, so that a spoon can glide through it easily at the dinner table.

1 Pour the milk into a heavy-bottomed pan, add 5½ oz/150 g of chocolate, and stir over medium heat for 3–5 minutes, or until melted. Remove from the heat and reserve.

2 Beat the egg yolks with all but 1 tablespoon of the sugar in a bowl until pale, then beat in the milk mixture, a little at a time. Transfer the mixture to a clean pan and cook over low heat, whisking, until smooth and thickened. Remove from the heat, let cool completely, then cover with plastic wrap. Chill for 30 minutes.

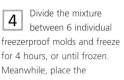

3 Whisk the egg whites and a pinch of salt in a clean, greasefree bowl until soft peaks form. Gradually whisk in the remaining sugar until stiff and glossy. Remove the chocolate mixture from the refrigerator and stir in the honey. Fold in the egg whites.

4 Divide the mixture between 6 individual freezerproof molds and freeze for 4 hours, or until frozen. Meanwhile, place the remaining chocolate in a heatproof bowl set over a pan of barely simmering water. Stir until melted and smooth, then dip the strawberries in the melted chocolate to half-coat them. Let set. Transfer the ice cream to the refrigerator 10 minutes before serving. Turn out on to serving plates and decorate with the strawberries.

index